SOME REAL PEOPLE'S RESPONSES:

The title of Karens latest companion workbook really says it all. *Take a Step with Him…Adventuring with God into Fresh Beginnings.* All it takes is one tiny step forward…a step of faith, and an exciting adventure will begin to unfold. Take that small step and begin the journey of a lifetime. As you immerse yourself in Karen's treasure chest of suggestions and tried and true ideas, you will be transformed and changed beyond measure. So take a deep breath and step out. You will be so glad you did.

Julie Jones

As I journey with the author on her walk with the Holy Spirit, I feel a longing arise within me to walk step by step with the Spirit, letting Him speak into my everyday situations and interactions.

I love how the Holy Spirit reveals insights to the author that allow her to minister to those she comes in contact with. I long to be more aware of the Spirit's leading as well. Too often, we feel the Spirit leading, and we resist, and over time, we become less attuned to His guidance. Or we have so much noise in our lives that we don't even hear Him. That is what makes this book so great. It will awaken in you, the reader, a desire to tune into the Spirit, to listen for His leading, and to obey.

Quoting from Father's Heart in chapter 10, 'My Spirit will guide you to the best teaching for your circumstances, which will help you to step out in My freedom once more.' This quote sums up this book for me, as God used the teaching in this book to call me to grow deeper in my relationship with Him.

Deb Chatley

Walking with Jesus is a day-by-day, moment-by-moment experience. He takes us one step at a time teaching us how to live like Him. While it's different for each of us, when we share these experiences, others can identify with it and take a step in their own life. *Take a Step* with Karen in her new devotional with a companion workbook and you'll find yourself a step closer to Jesus.

Mandy Farmer, Chronic Pain Author & Blogger at www.mandyfarmer.com

I have read a plethora of books with discussion questions that fall flat so I don't have high expectations for those. However, Karen's guidebook blew me away with her intentionality and superb connection to the Father, bringing His heart directly to each reader.

First of all, it is so much more than just a list of questions. The questions included are poignant, truly engaging the reader in processing each chapter thoroughly. The guidebook is also filled with relatable Scripture, prayers, important quotes from the chapter, playlists, and activations to bring the concept to life. I have not seen anything like it. You can tell Karen poured her heart into these companion books just as much as the main books. If you truly want to step into life with Jehovah this series with the guidebooks is the way to do it. Don't hesitate!

Sonya Loso

TAKE A *Step* WITH *Him*

COMPANION GUIDEBOOK

BOOK 3

TAKE A *Step* WITH *Him*

COMPANION GUIDEBOOK

KAREN BROUGH
Written by a very natural girl and a supernatural God

THE HOLY BIBLE, NEW INTERNATIONAL VERSION®, NIV® Copyright © 1973, 1978, 1984, 2011 by Biblica, Inc.® Used by permission. All rights reserved worldwide.

Scripture quotations marked NLT are taken from the *Holy Bible*, New Living Translation, copyright © 1996, 2004, 2015 by Tyndale House Foundation. Used by permission of Tyndale House Publishers, Inc., Carol Stream, Illinois 60188. All rights reserved.

Scripture taken from the New King James Version®. Copyright © 1982 by Thomas Nelson. Used by permission. All rights reserved.

The ESV® Bible (The Holy Bible, English Standard Version®). ESV® Text Edition: 2016. Copyright © 2001 by Crossway, a publishing ministry of Good News Publishers. The ESV® text has been reproduced in cooperation with and by permission of Good News Publishers. Unauthorized reproduction of this publication is prohibited. All rights reserved.

NASB New American Standard Bible®, Copyright © 1960, 1971, 1977, 1995, 2020 by The Lockman Foundation. All rights reserved.

Scripture quotations marked TPT are from The Passion Translation®. Copyright © 2017, 2018, 2020 by Passion & Fire Ministries, Inc. Used by permission. All rights reserved.

ThePassionTranslation.com. Holman Christian Standard Bible® Copyright © 1999, 2000, 2002, 2003, 2009 by Holman Bible Publishers. Used with permission by Holman Bible Publishers, Nashville, Tennessee. All rights reserved.

The Holy Scriptures Jubilee Bible 2000 (JUB) Copyright © 2013, 2020 Translated and Edited by Russell M. Stendal NET Bible® copyright ©1996-2017 All rights reserved.

Build 30170414 by Biblical Studies Press, L.L.C. Copyright © 1995, 2003, 2013, 2014, 2019, 2020 by God's Word to the Nations Mission Society. All rights reserved.

The Holy Bible, Berean Study Bible, BSB Copyright ©2016, 2020 by Bible Hub Used by Permission. All Rights Reserved Worldwide.

Copyright © 2023 By Karen Brough
karenbrough.com

Disclaimer: Although this publication is designed to provide accurate information in regard to the subject matter covered, the publisher and the author assume no responsibility for errors, inaccuracies, omissions, or any other inconsistencies herein. This publication is meant as a source of valuable information for the reader, however it is not meant as a replacement for direct expert assistance. If such level of assistance is required, the services of a competent professional should be sought.

All rights reserved. No part of this publication may be reproduced or transmitted in any form or by any means, electronic or mechanical, including photocopy, recording, or any information storage retrieval system, without permission in writing from the copyright owner.

ISBN 978-1-9229671-9-0 (paperback edition)
ISBN 978-0-6452451-1-0 (electronic edition)

To the ones who are unwilling to be defined by their circumstances; instead, taking God's hand and refusing to be separated from hope, this book is a tribute to you.

You don't always get a clappity doodah or a pat on the back for your perseverance and stickability...take this as your personal encouragement. You are cheered from the sidelines!

You are seen; your courage and your decision never to give up is acknowledged in this moment, sweet one of His.

You are doing an amazing job, and the lives of those around you are blessed by your example and touch.

Keep going, good things are just around the corner!

EDITOR

*(The ultimate language artist, accomplished, generous,
and precious new friend from across the oceans)*

Linda Stubblefield | affordablechristianediting.com

PROOFREADING AND EDITING GIFT-STRAIGHT FROM GOD.

Wise, empathetic, intuitive, and Father's heart girl,
Julie Jones, God bless you and yours, chickadee.

GRAPHIC CONCEPT DESIGN

*(The intuitive, talented creative heart
and developer of dreams)*

Abigail Parker | abigail@sponge.com.au

MAP ILLUSTRATOR

*(The courageous, gifted, illustrative visionary
and Holy Spirit led, heart woman of His)*

Stacey Leitch | staceyleitch.com

BOOK COVER DESIGN & FORMATTING

*(The oh so patient, professional, full of integrity,
skilled book creative and design king)*

Steve Kuhn | kuhndesigngroup.com

Contents

Letter to the Reader 11

Map 12

1. Testimony: *The Power of Your Story* 17

2. Forgiveness: *Time to Fly Free* 35

3. Opposite: *No Longer a Victim to What Comes at Me* 55

4. Blessing: *The Power of Our Words* 73

5. Prophetic Words: *God's Encouragement to Us* 93

6. Prophetic Acts: *Tangible, Symbolic Acts with Punch* 111

7. Joy: *Is It Really Possible in All Circumstances?* 129

8. Intercession: *Praying Like Jesus* 145

9. Looking Beyond Myself: *An Unselfish Life* 165

10. Sound Teaching: *Reinforcing Lasting Foundations for Life* 181

11. The Word: *Building on the Rock* 199

12. Visions: *Living Pictures, God's Gift through Visions* 215

13. Dreams: *Night Times and God Adventures as We Sleep* 233

14. Thankfulness: *Attitude of Gratitude Plants Much* 251

15. Lament: *How to Move Past Pain, by Honoring and Grieving Well* 271

16. Living Legacy: *God's Legacy Is His Gift to Me* 289

Bonus Chapter: *Adoration of God* 307

Bonus Chapter: *Adoration of Him* 311

APPENDICES

Appendix 1: Glossary 313

Appendix 2: Prayer Starters 315

Appendix 3: Blessing/Cursing 317

Appendix 4: Joy 319

Appendix 5: The Word 321

Appendix 6: Dreams 323

Explanation of the Autumn Leaf on the Cover 327

For Those on a Spiritual Journey Who Want to Connect
with God for Themselves 329

About the Author 333

Connect with Us 335

A Final Word 337

LETTER TO THE READER

Precious reader,

If you've reached this final book in the Be Held By Him series, I know that you will be seeing, hearing and experiencing God in ways that will bless your daily life.

This final book is designed to

- Invest further hope
- Stir the desire to start afresh in your present situation
- Learn more ways to connect with God for yourself
- Clear the house of the heart a little by processing your past, and asking God for His vision of the present and future

Take heart, there is always more to encounter of God, and what a bizarre and incredible thing it is; we will never reach the end of this experience.

My encouragement to you is this: dive in!

If it's good…
If it reflects His heart…
If it is aligned with Scripture and Jesus' model,
Dive in! Go for it!

What's stopping you from relishing life as fully as you can in this place you find yourself? Hindrances or not, God has ways for you to flourish—right now. And that, beloved reader, is my prayer for you—That you would flourish with Him.

And on the days where you feel it's beyond you, that you would allow Him to replenish, restore and encourage you. Thank you for going on this journey with me.

If you have enjoyed these books, I write and share many more God stories at karenbrough.com and through social media.

I look forward to cheering you on through these mediums.

Much love
Karen. *xxxxx*

The Journey

EXPLANATION OF THE MAP

"The Journey" map outlines the various chapters of each book in the *Be Held by Him* series.

He brought across my path the gifted illustrator, Stacey Leitch. She understood the subject matter personally and the moment we spoke, I knew she would be the right person for the work.

We've brainstormed together, and she's brought the conversations, God's instruction and her vision into something that continues to speak to me daily. *God bless you and your gift, Stacey.*

"The Journey" reveals a story of how God speaks to and interacts with us, especially in the hard seasons of life.

I pray it encourages you and invests hope in you.

There is always so much more to look forward to with God by your side.

Don't give up!

A QUICK PROVISO:

You might notice as you read that I don't use the traditional term "the Holy Spirit." I do not include the article "the." This choice is a personal one for me, and by no means do I wish to cause offense to anyone who thinks differently.

Each part of God—Father, Jesus, and Holy Spirit—is tangible, alive, and personable. Each is complete in themselves, but each connects with me in different ways.

For me to address "Holy Spirit" as "the Holy Spirit" would be to hold Him at a distance, and I want Him as near as possible. Please, feel free to add "the" if that designation fits with how you communicate with Him.

Bless you, precious one.

xxxxx

THIS COMPANION GUIDEBOOK IS A DOING BOOK.

This guidebook is not just another book to read; it is a doing book—Within its pages, you will find various ways in which God's wisdom, songs, verses, and activations transformed thinking, shifted atmospheres, and provided tangible encounters with our Mighty God, Loving Jesus, and Empowering Holy Spirit.

JOURNEY MAP:

The journey map provided in this guidebook will serve as your compass, revealing the numerous ways in which God can speak and connect with each of us at any given time. It encompasses the three books in this series and their chapters, offering guidance and hope, especially if you find yourself in a desert space right now. Take heart, for there is an abundance of goodness awaiting you.

PURPOSE AND IDENTITY:

During times when everything seemed disconnected and battles raged on, I embarked on a search for purpose, hope, and identity. It was during these moments that God made Himself known to me through the following avenues. Furthermore, I consciously chose to reach up to Him and invite Him into the mystery of my life, understanding that relationship is a two-way street.

INTIMACY WITH FATHER GOD:

My deepest hope for this book is that it fosters a greater intimacy between you and Father God. May its pages inspire you, tend to you, and enable powerful encounters as you choose to reach out and interact with the One who knows every step you take. He desires to bring you hope, purpose, light, and a level of faith that surpasses anything you have experienced before.

Much love
Karen
xxxxx

Chapter One

TESTIMONY

> Since we believe human testimony, surely we can believe the greater testimony that comes from God. And God has testified about his Son.
>
> I JOHN 5:9 NLT

To strengthen those crushed by despair who mourn in Zion—
to give them a beautiful bouquet in the place of ashes,
the oil of bliss instead of tears,
and the mantle of joyous praise
instead of the spirit of heaviness.
Because of this, they will be known as
Mighty Oaks of Righteousness,
planted by Yahweh as a living display of his glory.

ISAIAH 61:3 TPT

— Father's Heart —

I know that you've endured so much, My child. I was with you.

I know you have had some difficult beginnings and find yourself in challenging circumstances. My heart is grieved by the injustices and disappointments you have experienced.

I chose you to come into this world for such a time as this. You are no mistake, and what you've experienced will not be wasted.

I have travelled with you and comforted you during the storms, knowing a time would come where the things you have had to endure would accomplish My good purposes. Yes, even from within it.

I wish to tell you that none of these are wasted in Me. Your story and experiences will be used mightily in My name.

I want to redeem those very things that have held you back, pulled you down, or sought to steal your very future from you.

I have the power, ability, and desire to do this for you because I love you.

You are My child and I love you deeply.

The thing that looks to steal from you is the very thing I wish to redeem for you. I will show you the way I walk and work in this as you release it all to Me. Trust Me, precious child.

Trust Me with your past, your present, and your future.

Trust Me with the ups and downs. Trust Me in the bad news, the life shocks and troubles, as I am ever-present, ready to partner with you and bring you all that you need at any given moment.

My testimony of your life is very, very different to how it feels in the moment.

When you find yourself reflecting upon current challenges or past struggles, stop. Take a moment. Breathe with Me. Ask Me how I see the very thing that captivates your thoughts.

Let Me take your hand and help you to take the next step forward. It won't always be comfortable, but I do promise you that I will be with you. You won't ever be alone. I promise you that these very things sent to take your eyes off Me will strengthen our relationship—if you'll let Me in.

Those hard things will accomplish great things through Me.

My heart loves to beat to the tune of Redeemer, Redeemer, Redeemer because that is exactly Who I am. And it is exactly what I love to do for you, beloved.

Let Me share with you how I've been by your side all along. Let Me reveal to you how your story connects with Mine.

Our stories together make for redemptive, sweet, and joyous living.

Come, delight of My heart! Let's walk awhile together, and I will show you marvellous things that will lighten your load and uplift your heart.

TESTIMONY

— Take Aways —

God has a testimony of my life that I don't always see.

What I see and experience is only one layer of what is actually happening; God has a perfect vision of my true reality.

OTHERS' TESTIMONIES CAN HELP GIVE ME HOPE FOR MY CURRENT CIRCUMSTANCES.

I see with flawed, limited vision at times, but God never does.

Hearing myself tell of God's goodness makes holy transactions in tough times.

God has much in store for me and the future.

Being vulnerable in sharing testimonies helps to invest hope in others and lifts my own spirit.

My pain, hurt, and experiences will not be wasted.

My story is important; His story in me is powerful!

ALIGNING MY SIGHT WITH HIS IS ALWAYS THE BEST.

God's story of my life is better than I could imagine for myself.

TESTIMONY

Kingdom vision (God's testimony) reflects His heart, His nature and the fruit of His Spirit. It's the place I want to be as often as possible.

WORDS OF TESTIMONY HELP INVEST HOPE FOR THE FUTURE

God's testimony is one that is redemptive and whole.

God loves to take the broken things and restore their value.

What I tell myself about my story can set moods, tones, and outcomes for the future.

Seeking God in all things creates a life-changing shift for anything that comes at me.

— *Questions to Ponder* —

1. Was there anything that leapt out as I read this chapter about testimony?

2. What is the testimony I have of my own story? What are the highlights? What kinds of events/life experiences come to mind as I ponder this?

3. What influences my view of my story? Consider childhood, personality, environmental factors, significant events, education, etc.

4. What do I believe about my life testimony—both positive and negative?

> Praise be to the exalted Lord God of Israel, for he has seen us through eyes of grace, and he comes as our Hero-God to set us free!
>
> **LUKE 1:68 TPT**

5. What are the connections between life events and my mind? What does the Word tell me about this?

6. Does the way I look at my life and how God does differ, in any way?

7. What biblical evidence is there that God has a redemptive view of my story?

8. As I reflect upon life, is it my story, or God's and my story together, or God's story of which I am a part? Why do I believe this?

> But because the Lord loves you, and because He would keep the oath which He swore to your fathers, the Lord has brought you out with a mighty hand, and redeemed you from the house of bondage, from the hand of Pharaoh king of Egypt.
>
> **DEUTERONOMY 7:8 NKJV**

9. What is God's testimony of my current situation? How have I seen His hand at work in it? Ask Him more about this if I'm unsure.

10. How would it benefit this current season to see this circumstance through His eyes? How would it be advantageous to learn the rhythm of seeing life through God's sight?

> And we know that God causes everything to work together for the good of those who love God and are called according to his purpose for them.
>
> **ROMANS 8:28 NLT**

TESTIMONY

—Playlist—

"My Testimony" – Elevation Worship

"My Everything" – Owl City

"Revival Anthem" – Rend Collective

"Alive and Breathing: Song Session" – Matt Maher

"Hills and Valleys: Acoustic Session" – Tauren Wells

"This I Believe" – Hillsong

"Champion" – Maverick City

— Activations —

MUSICAL

Listen to "My Testimony" by Elevation Worship (Graves to Gardens album).

Ask Holy Spirit to remind you of a specific event where He invaded your world in a miraculous way—a time where He changed your life testimony from one thing to another. Create a piece of music or lyrics which share this testimony.

If you feel courageous enough to do so, share this composition with a safe person to spur them on in their faith.

VISUAL

Ask God to reveal a key moment where you knew God intervened in your situation—His testimony of your life. Now sculpt or create some memory stones to place around your home or garden as reminders of God's goodness. Take some time to revisit these often, especially when you need hope.

LOGICAL

Consider the life of Joseph and his family. Did they see the whole picture or what was hidden from them? What was their testimony?

TESTIMONY

Reread it, considering what God's testimony of Joseph's life might be. What elements are now present? Did this study change things for you as a reader? Why or why not? What do you observe about God's heart in this passage? What did you notice about your spirit as you read God's version? How could this help and/or apply to your current circumstance?

BODILY/KINESTHETIC

Consider a recent time where you've seen God at work in your life.

Move your body in ways that worship God. Giving Him thanks for all that He has done and is doing. Express thankfulness.

INTRAPERSONAL

Set apart some dedicated, unrushed, distraction free time with God.

Have a conversation with Him about your life's testimony.

How would you tell your story to someone? What events would make the list? What would be left out? How do you feel as you think upon life events?

Now ask God for His version of your life. Ask Him to reveal His hand in your life.

LINGUISTIC/VERBAL

Put the timer on for two minutes. Write a list of life events, moments, or circumstances. Create a helicopter view of your life's testimony.

Now do the same thing again, but this time ask God to share His testimony of your life with you. Spend some time pondering these with Him.

INTERPERSONAL

Spend some time with Holy Spirit or another trusted friend. Talk about what He brings to mind as you explain the influencing moments and experiences of life.

Spend some time praying and asking God for His version of your life. Take note of any words or pictures He gives you.

NATURALISTIC

Consider the theme of perspective.

How is vision expanded or limited in nature?

In your opinion, what kind of creature or plant has the best vision? Why?

What can this exercise teach you about your own life and how you wish to see things?

Ask God to reveal an application for you in all that you've seen and considered.

TESTIMONY

— Bless You —

Bless you one who has a life filled with His testimonies.

Be blessed as you encounter the love of the Father in fresh ways.

Be blessed with the hope that all you have walked through is not wasted.

Bless you with a pace of rest as you tune in to His testimony of your life.

God bless you with the greater testimony of God evidenced in your heart and mind.

Bless you with the knowledge that the redemptive hand of God is always with you at every turn.

I bless you with His vision to see all the freeing and beautiful things He is bringing to you at this time.

In the redemptive, powerful, loving name of Jesus Christ,

Amen.

xxxxx

Chapter Two

FORGIVENESS

Be kind to one another, tenderhearted, forgiving one another, as God in Christ forgave you.

EPHESIANS 4:32 ESV

— Father's Heart —

I have come that you might have life and life to the full.

Sin and poor choices are the world's currency;
My currency is higher, which lives above these things.

Time to release the old and make way for the new.

My precious child, I have forgiven you freely. I have released you from those heavy chains of burden. You no longer have to live under the weight of them.

You're aware of My higher way. You've come to Me and asked for forgiveness which I've given to you freely.

Why then, do you hold on to those things that I have already forgiven you for?

My precious Son Jesus died for those things, so you didn't have to live under them.

Why do you take back those things from which I have freed you?

Is it because you want to feel the pain, as if you deserve to remain in judgment?

I speak words that lift - like, "I judge you no more. I've forgiven you wholly." You've turned from your ways, and yet you sometimes choose to remember the mistakes you've made.

*If you are willing, let Jesus be Jesus! You don't need to
take His place in carrying sin and payment.*

As I forgive you, then surely you can also forgive yourself.

Let go of those things that Jesus forgave you for and has now released.

Let go of your right to hold something against yourself, My beloved.

Stop punishing yourself for things I will never remember.

*To receive something good in exchange, release
one thing that is holding you back.*

*Know that Jesus died so you didn't have to hold onto mistakes of the
past—those things that impact the present and can steal from the future.*

*It's time to give yourself the compassion and mercy that Jesus
has given you…and that you often give to others willingly.*

Be kind to yourself as you are kind to others and as Jesus is kind to you.

*Throw off the former in order to dance freely into fresh
beginnings. Step into wide open spaces, where you've been
forgiven, you forgive others, and yourself, freely.*

FORGIVENESS

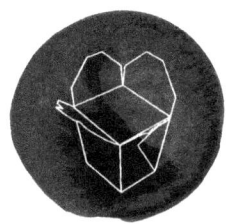

— *Take Aways* —

God reveals when forgiveness is needed, sometimes through conviction, and sometimes by making me aware that I am being reactive or triggered by people and situations.

Jesus keeps my heart focused and sure on healthy relationships.

FORGIVENESS IS A POWER KEY TO FREEDOM.

God desires forgiveness for my benefit as well as others.

If Jesus has forgiven me with all my flaws and mistakes, then I can forgive others.

God is my defender and judge when I've been wronged. Am I willing to release these offenses to Him?

Forgiveness is about my living offense free, loving well, and having an unhindered relationship with God.

UNFORGIVENESS HURTS ME AND OTHERS.

God is the One with Whom I can share my deepest regrets and mistakes and receive forgiveness myself.

Jesus is the reason I can forgive.

FORGIVENESS

Freedom from shame, fear and so many other strongholds can be disempowered with forgiveness.

FORGIVENESS LIGHTENS THE LOAD AND RELEASES BURDENS.

Forgiving someone doesn't mean I approve of behaviour.

Forgiveness restores much and costs little.

My heart can't ignore unforgiveness; it's impacted by it.

Is there angst, unrest, or a lack of peace within? Asking God if there is someone or something I need to forgive is healthy practice.

— Questions To Ponder —

1. Was there anything that I want to note down about forgiveness?

2. What do I believe about forgiveness? What is its purpose? Who is it for?

3. Why forgive? What happens if I don't? Is there any situation where unforgiveness is acceptable?

4. What is the connection between Jesus and forgiveness? What do I believe God's intention is for forgiveness? Does God "need" me to forgive others? Will it change Him in any way? Who does forgiveness benefit?

5. Has there been a significant time when I forgave someone? What do I remember about that situation? What did I experience physically before and after I'd chosen to forgive?

6. What happens if I am not forgiven by others? What can I do about this? How can I respond? What do I notice about relationships when this lack of forgiveness is evident?

> Therefore there is now no condemnation at all for those who are in Christ Jesus.
>
> **ROMANS 8:1 NKJV**

7. When have I experienced forgiveness? What did I experience internally before and after someone had forgiven me?

8. What happens if I choose not to forgive? Are there any consequences if I hold on to unforgiveness? What, if any, is the fruit of failing to forgive?

> Therefore confess your sins to each other and pray for each other so that you may be healed. The prayer of a righteous person is powerful and effective.
>
> **JAMES 5:16 NIV**

9. When I feel as though I can't forgive, what kinds of things might I believe? What can help me? Does this align with God's vision of life?

10. Practically speaking, how do I forgive—especially when it feels unforgivable? Is there anyone I feel I need to forgive today?

> He does not punish us for all our sins; he does not deal harshly with us, as we deserve. For his unfailing love toward those who fear him is as great as the height of the heavens above the earth.
>
> **PSALM 103:10-11 NLT**

FORGIVENESS

11. What benefits does forgiveness bring to my life as well as the lives of others? What advantages might forgiveness bring to my current situation?

> Repent therefore and be converted, that your sins may be blotted out, so that times of refreshing may come from the presence of the Lord, and that He may send Jesus Christ, who was preached to you before, whom heaven must receive until the times of restoration of all things, which God has spoken by the mouth of all His holy prophets since the world began.
>
> **JAMES 3:19 NKJV**

Tolerate the weaknesses of those in the family
of faith, forgiving one another in the same
way you have been graciously forgiven by Jesus
Christ. If you find fault with someone, release
this same gift of forgiveness to them. For love
is supreme and must flow through each of these
virtues. Love becomes the mark of true maturity.
Let your heart be always guided by the peace
of the Anointed One, who called you to peace as
part of his one body. And always be thankful.

COLOSSIANS 3:13-15 TPT

FORGIVENESS

—Playlist—

"Holy Water" – We the Kingdom

"Rise Up" – Matt Maher

"The Broken Beautiful" – Ellie Holcomb

"Amazing God" – Brenton Brown

"Letting Go" – Steffany Gretzinger

"Hymn of Heaven: Song Session" – Phil Wickham

"Dancing on the Waves – We the Kingdom

— Activations —

MUSICAL

With Holy Spirit, ask for a line of truth about forgiveness.

Quietly wait for this truth to land within you. Consider what He shares and what it means.

As He prompts, pick up your instrument, pen, or ready your voice and express this revelation in worship.

VISUAL

Consider Jesus' ultimate act of love and the grace He gave us in return.

What is the primary emotion you feel as you become aware of the grace you've been given? Represent this in your own way. Create a Jesus-inspired piece/picture of forgiveness or grace.

LOGICAL

Research the verses which pertain to forgiveness. Note them down. Categorise and group them as you see fit. Consider the consequences of choosing to forgive or not.

What does the Word say to us about each choice? How can this be applied in your own life?

BODILY/KINESTHETIC

Spend some time with God. Follow His leading and the first thoughts He gives.

Become aware of how your body responds to:

- God forgiving you.
- You are forgiven.
- Forgiving yourself.
- Forgiving others.

Take note of what happens in your body as you do.

What do you observe about the impact of forgiveness upon your organs and body systems?

Thoughts? Feelings? Senses?

INTRAPERSONAL

Set apart some time to do a forgiveness stocktake with God.

Seek God's insight into the following:

- Is there anyone I need to forgive?
- Is there anyone I have injured?
- Is there anything for which I need to forgive myself?
- How do I know I have forgiven someone wholly?
- Am I willing to go on a process with God and forgiveness?
- What does Jesus say about forgiveness to me?

LINGUISTIC/VERBAL

Write a creative story or poem which weaves in your own experience with God's truth about forgiveness and grace. Consider using specific verses as inspiration and basis for this work.

INTERPERSONAL

Spend some time with a trusted friend or Christian counsellor.

Let this be a time of seeking God's heart about events and people.

Are there things for which I need to forgive myself?
Are there people I need to forgive?

Are there things for which I need to ask God for forgiveness?

NATURALISTIC

Collect some firewood, twigs, and brush. Safely set up a small campfire.

As you watch the flames flicker, thank God for whatever comes to mind. Ask Him to reveal anyone you need to forgive. Write these on small notes.

As you bring these before God, repenting or forgiving, toss each one into the fire as a symbolic act of faith. Enjoy the freedom and quiet of the crackling fire with Him.

FORGIVENESS

— Bless You —

Bless you one who is wholly forgiven and can forgive as a result.

Be blessed with an encounter with God's grace today.

Bless you with encountering the abundant love of Jesus.

God bless you with a soft heart and His protection of it.

May you have courage to forgive those who have injured you.

Be blessed with fully releasing pain, offense, and upset to Him.

Bless you with the ability to trust Him above all else.

May you have freedom to own when you've made mistakes and willingness to help heal when you've hurt others. Ask for forgiveness and the wisdom to walk in His ways.

God bless you with a kind heart, forgiving one another, just as Christ forgave you.

May you encounter the truth that nothing can separate you from the love of God.

God bless you with the realization that forgiveness leads to freedom.

In the beautifully forgiving and redemptive name of Jesus Christ,

Amen.

xxxxx

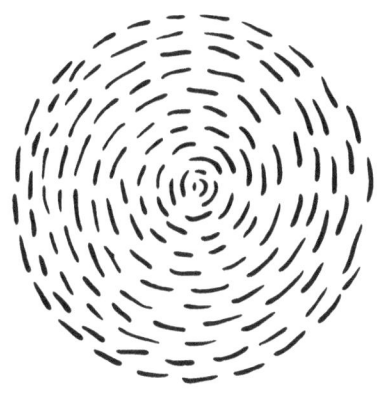

Chapter Three

OPPOSITE

But I tell you, love your enemies and pray
for those who persecute you, that you may
be children of your Father in heaven.

MATTHEW 5:44-45A NIV

— Father's Heart —

When the troubles of this world come, and they will, what will you choose to believe? My truth or the lies of the prince of heaviness?

My Spirit is everything about My heart and nature that is good, because I am good.

When I tell you that I am good, it means there is nothing bad about Me; think about this attribute for a moment.

I love it when you spend time with Me and get to know Me.

Out of this time spent with Me, you develop a foundation for knowing when something is from Me or opposed to My heart.

Know Me, and you will know absolute freedom.

There is a way to walk in life that is higher and lovelier than you could ever imagine!

Cast off those things that do not reflect My heart of goodness. They are not a good fit for you; they were never destined for you to address alone.

With Me, it is possible to have peace in times of angst.

With Me, it is possible to have love for someone even when they have crushed your heart.

With Me, it is possible to forgive the unforgivable and be free.

With Me, it is possible, it is possible, it IS possible! All things are possible with Me.

I have a stream of living water available to you right now.

Step into the cool, refreshing flow of peace with Me.

Dip your toe into the current that teams with My life-giving Spirit.

Do not swim against My tide anymore, My child! That way of swimming depletes your resources.

I have a way for you to move and live in freedom, whatever comes at you.

Whatever the enemy throws at you is not beyond you — because I am with you.

I have plans that will shake off those things, lifting you up to your rightful status—as an overcomer—with Me.

It's time to cast off those chains which have been hanging around your neck—and dive into the waters which bring life to your bones and sweetness to your life song.

This is My current and My currency for You because I love you and want you to be free. A flow which fills, blesses and lightens. Where there is an absence of these things, stop. What is the opposite of the negative, weighty, burden that comes at you? Then ask Me for what you need.

I long to give it to you.

OPPOSITE

— Take Aways —

Humanly speaking, if something is burdensome, overwhelming, anxiety or depression-causing, if there is angst, fear or frustration, God is offering a gift of the opposite.

Opposite walking directly impacts the atmosphere and those around me.

I always have a choice. I am not at the whim of my circumstance.

WHEN FEAR STRIKES, GOD HAS PEACE AVAILABLE FOR ME.

Whatever I find creeping in and destroying My mindset of peace or life, start speaking, praying and walking in the opposite spirit of whatever is coming at me.

Choosing the higher road draws my soul up into kingdom territory.

CHAPTER THREE

When afflictions or symptoms arise, God has health, healing, strength and peace for me to draw upon.

God's ways crush the challenges often in the opposite way of what I'm experiencing.

Honoring others despite how they behave speaks loudly about the position of my heart.

Honoring and blessing those who curse me aligns me with God's kingdom ways.

Stepping out in the opposite spirit to what is coming against me can be freeing.

Kingdom vision impacts the atmosphere as I draw near to His nature and heart.

WALKING IN HIS WAY WELCOMES AND DRAWS BLESSING TO ME.

Difficult relationships, battered hearts, weary bodies, conflicted mind? God has something that is the complete opposite of these.

OPPOSITE

Challenging, hard, weighty, negative, unhealthy feelings and experiences can be combated by coming at them in the opposite of them (See Appendix 1).

Whatever comes, God has antidotes, answers, and strategies; I am never without Him or His solutions.

GOD'S SPIRIT IS OPPOSITE TO THE ENEMY

When anxiety comes, God has faith to impart to me.

In the process of choosing to walk in the opposite of what is coming at me, He can redeem them, it, or me.

Activating the opposite can go against the grain of what "feels" natural.

Whatever steals peace or joy and whatever destroys healthy mindsets or distracts from life… start praying the opposite of these. (see appendix 1)

— *Questions to Ponder* —

1. Was there anything that leapt out about activating the opposite?

2. What does it mean to function in the opposite spirit or to activate the opposite?

3. Are there any Bible passages which reflect this idea of opposite? What is it about these Scriptures that jump out?

4. If I were to describe the nature of God, what aspects would I include?

> When a man's ways are pleasing to the Lord, he makes even his enemies live at peace with him.
>
> **PROVERBS 16:7 ESV**

CHAPTER THREE

5. If God has solutions to every plan of the enemy, what would God's characteristics combat? What does He provide for me?

6. What area of my life do I feel compelled to walk in the opposite way? Why or why not? (Refer to Appendix 1 for prompts.)

> The sinful nature wants to do evil, which is just the opposite of what the Spirit wants. And the Spirit gives us desires that are the opposite of what the sinful nature desires. These two forces are constantly fighting each other, so you are not free to carry out your good intentions.
>
> **GALATIANS 5:17 NLT**

OPPOSITE

7. How comfortable am I with walking opposite to what is coming at me? What might help me combat this? Ask God for a strategy.

8. Have I experienced walking in the opposite way in my life? When? What did God ask me to step into, walk, or declare instead of it? What was the outcome? What is an every-day example of this?

> God has not given us a spirit of fear, but of power and of love and of a sound mind.
>
> **2 TIMOTHY 1:7 NKJV**

9. What benefits might walking in the way God reveals instead of what I feel or see, have for my current situation?

___

> That's why I take pleasure in my weaknesses,
> and in the insults, hardships, persecutions,
> and troubles that I suffer for Christ. For
> when I am weak, then I am strong.
>
> **2 CORINTHIANS 12:10 NLT**

Playlist

Where Feet May Fail – Hillsong Worship

Rise Up – Matt Maher

The Broken Beautiful – Ellie Holcomb

Amazing God – Brenton Brown

Lead Me to the Cross – Francesca Battistelli

I Will Exalt You – Dante Bowe

Yahweh Song Session – All Nations Music featuring Chandler Moore

— *Activations* —

MUSICAL

The next time you are emotionally heavy, burdened, or having your peace stolen, step into the exploration of worship which reflects the opposite of what you are feeling. Refer to Appendix 1 for ideas. If you aren't in this space, consider interceding for someone God brings to mind with the opposite of what they are walking through.

VISUAL

Look at Appendix 1 and ask Holy Spirit to highlight an opposite that fits for your current circumstances, watch for something that leaps out to you. Create a piece that reflects the light and dark of the theme He highlighted.

LOGICAL

Study the biblical evidence supporting walking in the opposite way. What does it reveal? What are the relationships between health and these things? What conclusions can you derive? How can you apply this to life?

BODILY/KINESTHETIC

Find a long path to walk. Consider any unhealthy, heavy circumstances you are walking at the moment. How do you feel as you think of these?

Symbolically drop these things at the start of the path.

Ask God what He wants to give you to combat it, i.e. what He wants to give you in exchange for the truth.

Turn and walk in the opposite way—away from what is burdening you in this time.

As you walk farther away from where you started, note how this impacts your feelings and physical body?

INTRAPERSONAL

What is your biggest internal challenge right now? What unhealthy response or habit has been a struggle for you? What does God have for you to combat this thing? How does He want you to apply it the next time it comes up? Refer to Appendix 1 for help. Formulate an action plan with Him.

LINGUISTIC/VERBAL

Using your life story, write a persuasive piece to encourage someone to step into the opposite of what is coming against them. Ensure you note the benefits within the piece.

INTERPERSONAL

Spend some time asking God if there is an area of your life where this key could be applied. Ask Him if there have been any habits, behaviours, responses or lies you've been believing that are stealing from you. Now ask Him what opposite He wants to gift you.

NATURALISTIC

Take some time to visit a local water source. Note how the currents work and what happens when something moves in opposition to the natural current. Consider the current being the way God designed us to walk through life. If you can, get into the water and walk with the current. Let Him reveal some truth to you about life today.

The Spirit of the Sovereign Lord is on me,
because the Lord has anointed me
to proclaim good news to the poor.
He has sent me to bind up the brokenhearted,
to proclaim freedom for the captives
and release from darkness for the prisoners,
to proclaim the year of the Lord's favour
and the day of vengeance of our God,
to comfort all who mourn,
and provide for those who grieve in Zion—
to bestow on them a crown of beauty
instead of ashes,
the oil of joy
instead of mourning,
and a garment of praise
instead of a spirit of despair.
They will be called oaks of righteousness,
a planting of the Lord
for the display of his splendour.

ISAIAH 61:1-3 NIV

Bless You

Bless you, one who is loved beyond measure:

God bless you with the peace that passes all understanding as you walk with Him.

Bless you with knowing when something is of God and when it is not.

May Jesus bless you with life, and life to the full.

Be blessed in experiencing God in every area where you have need.

Bless you with greater revelation of His capacity where you have limited capacity.

Be blessed with freedom and discernment when activating His opposite in life.

God bless you with your mountains being made low, and your valleys being raised up as you embrace His natural flow.

Bless your relationships and interactions with the kiss of heaven.

May grace drip from every word that comes from your mouth, every thought that enters your mind, and every cry that is released from your heart.

Be blessed, precious one of His, with true freedom in life.

Amen.

xxxxx

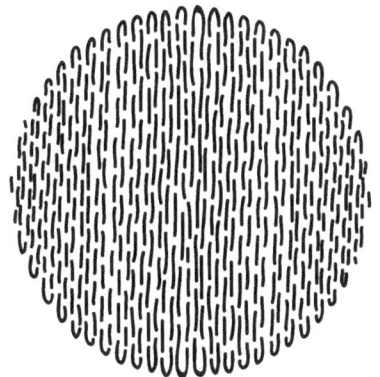

Chapter Four

BLESSING

*The tongue has the power of life and death,
and those who love it will eat its fruit.*

PROVERBS 18:21 NIV

— Father's Heart —

My Word is My blessing.

When you invite Me in, trusting Me with every situation, I will bring to it a redemptive thread.

My heart is to bless.

I love to bless My children.

I love to show them the depths of My love for them.

Not only does My blessing make you feel a small portion of My love for you; it also helps deepen your trust in Me.

When you choose to bless instead of curse, life is released.

I am Life.

When you speak words of blessing over someone, I am released to work in that person.

Blessing comes not as something deserved; rather, it is a result of My grace.

I bless you, not because of what you do, rather who you are to Me.

Trust Me to work all things for good.

When you choose to bless, the plans of any foe are obliterated, and they stand in confusion at your choice to bless.

I will turn every curse upon you into a blessing, as You choose to walk closely with Me.

Stand firm in My name. No matter what comes your way, My child, know that I am always with you. You are blessed, and you will continue to be blessed.

Even during hard times, I am always with you.

As I am with you, My abundance, love and answers are with you. These are all blessings.

When you feel like complaining, gossiping, speaking words of discontent, STOP.

Talk to Me about your worries. Invite Me into your circumstance and concern. Then become aware of My peace around and in you. As you become more aware of Me, you have an opportunity to see My life-giving perspective of what you are experiencing.

Every word you might have spoken in lack, now choose to declare the opposite, in love.

Declare blessing in My name, and I will show you how powerful I am.

BLESSING

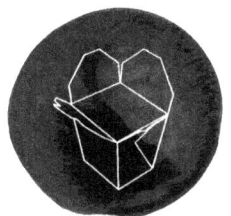

— Take Aways —

I can speak God's blessing over my body, relationships, marriages, communities, churches, nations, and the world.

If it's not uplifting and brings others down, then it might be time to start blessing them instead of cursing and watch what happens.

Blessing lifts the broken-hearted and tends to the afflicted.

Blessing welcomes in the storehouse of heaven as it aligns with a currency of heaven.

Blessing brings healing and wholeness to all areas of life.

GOD BLESSES ME, AND I CAN BLESS OTHERS.

As I align with the heart of God, blessing becomes a natural synchronous effect.

Blessing is a key of immeasurable force.

I have experienced breakthrough by blessing my body, rather than complaining about what isn't working.

Blessings are given through a variety of ways, words, actions, thoughts, prayers, intercession and so much more.

BLESSING IS A FOUNTAIN AND WELLSPRING OF LIFE.

Blessing is a language of heaven, and I want to speak that as often as I can.

I have only seen the tip of the iceberg when it comes to the revelation of speaking God's word in blessing.

BLESSING

Doing a life audit is a healthy practice. What words am I speaking? What thoughts am I fostering? Do I bless more than I curse?

BLESSING DEMOLISHES STRONGHOLDS AND RELEASES THE CAPTIVES.

There is great power in blessing.

Blessing is far more powerful than cursing. This is reason for great hope!

What if all I said, thought, and did, came to pass?

It's a healthy practice to ask God, "Are there any sources of cursing in my life?" Following up with asking what He wants to exchange it with is wonderful!

— *Questions to Ponder* —

1. What came to mind as I read about the power of words—blessing and cursing?

2. What do I believe about my words and speaking them out?

3. Have I experienced the sting of an unkind word or the blessing of life-giving words spoken by me or to me?

4. What impact have words had upon me in my life so far? What do I notice about the words I speak to myself and to others?

> But my God shall supply all your need according to his riches in glory by Christ Jesus.
>
> **PHILIPPIANS 4:19 KJV**

5. Are there areas where I find myself speaking lack or negativity? Are there any triggering themes or lies which are revealed through my speech? Ask Holy Spirit for clarity about this.

6. How do I respond to unwelcome words spoken by others? How do I process these? Am I able to let them go? What does God say about how to respond?

> The point is this: whoever sows sparingly will also reap sparingly, and whoever sows bountifully will also reap bountifully.
>
> **2 CORINTHIANS 9:6 ESV**

7. How do I manage the tension of wanting the blessing that comes from kingdom speech, and living in a culture that doesn't always abide by kingdom ways (myself included)?

8. What can the hearing of kind words of blessing do to my internal state—my heart, mind, and spirit? What is one healthy strategy that can be applied in my life? What is the first step in this?

CHAPTER FOUR

9. What place does God have in respect to my thoughts and speech? Do I consider Him and His words in my life? How can I apply them more readily?

10. What blessings does the Bible have for me? How can I adopt and walk in these daily?

> Bless those who curse you, pray for those who mistreat you.
>
> **LUKE 6:28 NIV**

11. How might my relationships allow blessing to flow from my lips? (instead of anything else)

12. What benefits might I experience if I chose to keep blessing at the forefront of my heart and mind?

> I call heaven and earth to witness against you today, that I have set before you life and death, the blessing and the curse. So choose life in order that you may live, you and your descendants.
>
> **DEUTERONOMY 30:19 NASB**

The Lord bless you and keep you; the Lord make His face to shine upon you and be gracious to you; the Lord lift up his countenance upon you and give you peace.

NUMBERS 6:24-26 ESV

BLESSING

—Playlist—

The Blessing – Chris Brown, Cody Carnes, Kari Jobe, Steve Furtick

Counting Every Blessing – Rend Collective

Limitless, Acoustic version – Colton Dixon

From Whom All blessings Flow – Doxology

This I Believe – Hillsong

Speak Life – Toby Mac

We Speak Life – Planetshakers

— Activations —

MUSICAL

With Holy Spirit, spend time blessing whoever comes
to mind; bless them in music and song.

VISUAL

Collect your favourite creative mediums.

Consider what blessing looks and feels like.

Ask God for inspiration for your heart. (See Appendix 2—"A Gift from Jesus.")

Represent this idea of blessing.

LOGICAL

Carry out the strawberry experiment. (I have since
heard it works with cooked rice as well.)

Place three look-alike strawberries in three separate ziplock/sandwich
bags: one for blessing, one for cursing, and one to ignore.

Make observations, take photographs of each of the berries each day.
What did you notice? Did they change? Did it have the expected results?
What did you learn? How might this experiment apply to life?

BLESSING

BODILY/KINESTHETIC

Ask Holy Spirit how you might bless your body today. Take note of the first thought that comes to mind and follow through in doing that.

INTRAPERSONAL

What if every word that came out of your mouth came true? Would you still speak the same way? What would be the fruit of your words?

Take a thought and word inventory of what is coming into your mind and heart and out of your mouth.

LINGUISTIC/VERBAL

Select a meaningful and encouraging Scripture promise or passage.

Rewrite this as a blessing or declaration of hope and strength.

Extension: Create a deck of go-to blessing cards for encouragement.

Enjoy the truth that is released as He blesses you through the Word.

Share these with anyone God reveals to your heart.

INTERPERSONAL

Become aware of God's presence and choose to step into the heartbeat of God. Stop and take note of what Father God is saying to you. Who and what does He want you to bless? Bless with your mouth and your actions—all that is life-giving and life-affirming.

NATURALISTIC

Walk through your favourite garden area and collect a group of natural elements. Create a bouquet of blessing to enjoy or share it with someone special.

If you don't wish to pick anything, then photograph some elements of the natural world to which you feel drawn and share an image with a family member, friend, or neighbour.

Blessed is the man who remains steadfast under trial, for when he has stood the test he will receive the crown of life, which God has promised to those who love him.

JAMES 1:12 ESV

— Bless You —

Bless you, one who is blessed by God.

God bless you with kingdom insight in this area of blessing and cursing.

Be blessed with a heart that longs for God's blessing.

Bless your tongue with the wisdom to speak life.

Be blessed with Holy Spirit's wisdom and discernment in knowing how to align with God's provision and blessing.

Bless you with courage to respond instead of react.

Be blessed with experiencing the fruit of your choice to speak, live, and think blessing.

Bless you with God's peace and the strength to bless those who persecute you.

We bless this season with vision that sees the benefits of blessing.

In the fruit-filled name of our blessed Jesus,

Amen.

xxxxx

Chapter Five

PROPHETIC WORDS

But the one who prophesies speaks to people for
their strengthening, encouraging and comfort.

1 CORINTHIANS 14:3 NIV

— Father's Heart —

My words never return to Me empty.

Are you weary, dry or wandering in the wilderness of life?

*Do you wonder where I am and what I would say
about all that you are walking through?*

*I have sweet words of hope which will be like honey
to your soul and healing balm for your heart.*

*My words always reflect My heart of love for you. My desire
is to bring you good things of encouragement and life.*

You need never fear the words I say; they are always for your good.

I have plans for a hope and future for you; My words will always reflect this.

*Prophetic words are simply words of encouragement and instruction
for you; they are markers, helpers, and something strategic.*

They are not orders or commands; that isn't My heart or nature.

*My words are invitations to partner with My heart. Will you join with My
plan for life? Will you choose the thing that I know will bring the best?*

I desire this for you, My precious one, because I love you.

Sometimes these words will come through My Word. They might be brought through My children. Other times they are given in creative ways.

*The way of communication is not as important
as the message I am releasing to you.*

Keep watch. Be aware of Me in the everyday.

Ask questions. Look out for Me, My darling. I am not hidden as you sometimes feel. I bring you messages of hope and delight constantly.

*It's My message melody, drawing you closer to Myself, investing
the very things that you need to take the next step.*

You are never alone because I am with you.

*Stop for a moment; become aware of Me in the noise. Be
still before Me and pick up My peace. From this awareness
of Me, you will begin to see Me in all things.*

*Life will unfold before you in miraculous and
empowering ways, through these words.*

My words draw you nearer to Me; anything else isn't Me.

*Look for the things that enable us to connect authentically with
one another. As you become aware of Me, you will learn to
recognise My sound, My nature, and My heart. I get great delight
as we connect with one another in this way, My beloved.*

PROPHETIC WORDS

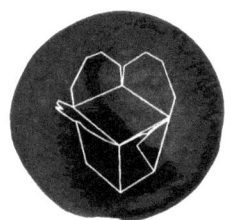

— *Take Aways* —

To give a word, I need to first know how I personally hear from God. (every chapter in the 'Be Held by Him,' book series is a different way God can communicate)

Before I give a word to someone, it's good etiquette to ask the person if he or she wants to hear the word. If not, shake the dust off your feet. If so, bless the person with the words He has given you.

PROPHETIC WORDS ARE GIVEN ONLY WITH THE HELP AND INSPIRATION OF HOLY SPIRIT.

The gift of prophecy is for everyone (Acts 2:16-21).

Prophets and prophecy aren't the same thing.

Prophecy requires a measure of courage, when we choose to step out in faith. Thankfully God helps us in this.

Prophecy is never to condemn or judge another person—only to reflect the heart of the Father.

At their core, prophetic words are encouragements from God.

Prophetic words allow others and me to practice hearing God.

PROPHETIC WORDS ARE LIKE LOVE LETTERS FROM GOD.

Through the Word, pictures, verses, scenes…God speaks in many, many ways.

PROPHETIC WORDS

If He gives a word of knowledge (a knowing of something personal about the person), asking what He wants to me to say is always a great place to begin.

THE WORD TELLS ME TO DESIRE THE GIFT OF PROPHECY.

If what He reveals isn't encouraging, edifying, or uplifting, then I need to ask some clarfying questions.

If the word is accurate, celebrate and give glory to God for His kindness.

Listening is a HUGE part of the prophetic.

When I share a word with someone, I try to phrase it in a way that gives them the option of receiving it as something from God. My saying, "God said…" demands the listener to agree. That phrasing can also feel pushy and not gentle.

— Questions to Ponder —

1. Was there anything about prophetic words that I'd like to note down?

2. What are prophetic words? What do I believe about them?

PROPHETIC WORDS

3. How would I explain what a prophetic word is without using the word prophetic? Try to explain it in simple language.

4. Have I ever received a prophetic word? How did I react to this experience?

> For we know in part and
> we prophesy in part.
>
> **1 CORINTHIANS 13:9 NIV**

5. What biblical examples can I find of prophetic words?

6. When someone is giving a prophetic word or encouragement from God, what elements should it bring? What does the Bible say about it?

> Concerning this salvation, the prophets, who spoke of the grace that was to come to you, searched intently and with the greatest care.
>
> **1 PETER 1:10 NIV**

7. How do I receive a prophetic word? What if I don't belong to a prophetic community of believers? Can God give me a prophetic word? How?

8. What if I don't agree with the word given? What can I do with that word? How should I test a word that is given?

9. What benefits or advantages could prophetic words bring to me in difficult seasons?

10. Do I agree with the following statement: "At their core, prophetic words are encouragement for the building up of an individual or church. They should reflect the Father's nature and Holy Spirit's fruit. They need to be edifying, encouraging or instructional and never instill fear, judgment or condemnation." Why or why not?

> Where there is no prophetic vision the people cast off restraint, but blessed is he who keeps the law.
>
> **PROVERBS 29:18 ESV**

PROPHETIC WORDS

Faith Is Rising – Jonathan David

Prophesy – Influence Music

Better Than – Bethel Music, featuring Jonathan David and Melissa Helser

Prophesy Your Promise – Bryan and Katie Towalt

You Are Beautiful Beyond Description – Maranatha Music

Promises – Maverick City Worship

The Battle Is Yours – Red Rocks Worship

— Activations —

MUSICAL

Rest with God for a moment; be still before Him. When you are aware of His presence or peace, ask Holy Spirit for a word, a phrase, a picture, or a sense—the starting point to inspire prophetic worship. Then play or write lyrics with Him in free, flowing creativity.

VISUAL

Use your artistic materials to create with Holy Spirit. Ask Him specifically for a word or a phrase for this season. He may even give you a picture that reflects the heart of what He wants to convey to your heart. Mirror this image, word, or phrase artistically. Let it be a time of listening to the Great Artist and His encouragement for you.

LOGICAL

Explore the area of prophecy in the word. Why is there conflict in the body of Christ about prophecy? What are the arguments on each side? Spend some time asking God for a revelation of truth about this difference of opinion.

PROPHETIC WORDS

BODILY/KINESTHETIC

Free dance with God. Close your eyes and ask God to reveal a prophetic dance or movement He wants you to express. Ask Holy Spirit to let the symbolism be evident in your heart as you move. It might also be an intercessory time through your movement. No doubt it'll be powerful however He leads you.

INTRAPERSONAL

Assuming you have a prophetic word, revisit them. If you do not have a word as yet, spend some time asking God for one. Keep watch for repeating words or themes in life and in everyday life—for things out of the ordinary. Ask God more about this.

LINGUISTIC/VERBAL

Take your writing materials to a quiet place. Ask God for a prophetic word or picture for you or for someone else. Then ask Him who each is for. Follow through with sending it to the person. It'll bless you and them. Write down phrases, words, or pictures He gives you.

INTERPERSONAL

Ask a friend if you could meet to pray and prophesy over one another. Keep in mind that prophetic words are encouragements from God. Plenty of books and activations are available about the prophetic if you are unfamiliar with this area.

NATURALISTIC

Ask Holy Spirit to reveal a prophetic word or message in nature. Keep watch for things that stand out to you and repeat in life. Pray into this, ask God about it, and if He wants to you do something in response.

FABULOUS RESOURCES FOR PROPHETIC:

Beth Kennedy | godisgoodstories.com
Features a solid prophetic base and teaching, including courses and others to connect with in the prophetic to learn and practice in safety.

Jane Berry | www.unlockingthegold.com
Unlocking the gold is full to the brim with activations and prophetic fun, inspiration, information and starting points.

> We also have the prophetic message as something completely reliable, and you will do well to pay attention to it, as to a light shining in a dark place, until the day dawns and the morning star rises in your hearts. Above all, you must understand that no prophecy of Scripture came about by the prophet's own interpretation of things. For prophecy never had its origin in the human will, but prophets, though human, spoke from God as they were carried along by the Holy Spirit.
>
> **2 PETER 1:19-21 NIV**

PROPHETIC WORDS

— Bless You —

*Be blessed, one whose Father has good plans
and words for you in this season.*

God bless you with His wisdom and discernment.

I bless you with timely words that speak life into your situation.

*Be blessed with words that bring clarity, confirmation,
and encouragement at this time.*

*I bless you in Jesus' name with words that speak to
the core of the unseen things of your heart.*

*That you would know, wholly, completely that God is for
you and has so much good in store for your future.*

In Jesus' powerful, freeing and healing name,

Amen.

xxxxx

Chapter Six

PROPHETIC ACTS

So he went down and dipped himself in the Jordan seven times, as the man of God had told him, and his flesh was restored and became clean like that of a young boy.

2 KINGS 5:14 NIV

— Father's Heart —

Trust Me—for I am trustworthy.

I have so much for us to do together that might involve your acting in ways that are not comfortable or logical.

I am bigger than human logic. I am greater than what is seen with the human eye. Whatever I ask will always align with My Father heart.

My heart is for you—not against you, My child.

I will not ask you to do anything beyond your capability or beyond what I have resourced you for.

When I ask you to do something in faith, trust Me to partner with you as you step forward in obedience.

If I have said it, if I have promised it, I will do this for you. Trust Me to know you and what you need best.

Sometimes I will ask you to intercede on behalf of a situation or a person in your life.

I will highlight them to you. Trust Me and be obedient to what I have placed on your heart. Then release it to Me and move on with the rest of the day.

If it reflects My good nature and the fruit of My Spirit, if it aligns with Jesus' model and My word…these are all sound measuring sticks.

Celebrate and thank Me for what I am doing because I am always doing something. That is the truth.

Many of you fear the people you see and what they might think of you.

Do not try to seek human approval, only Mine.

The truth is, you already have My approval.

You are amazing.

Nothing you do can make me love you any more than I do right now.

I love you completely—100 percent—and have done so since the beginning of time.

By choosing to be obedient to My call, our relationship is placed first and foremost in your life.

It brings Me joy to see you flourishing in union with Me.

When acting in faith, prophetic acts welcome a greater revelation of Myself into a person, place, or situation.

Release My truth into a situation, and I will display My glory and perfection within it, creating poetry before your eyes—astounding the eyes and hearts of the scoffers whom you once feared.

The truth of My heavenly realm infiltrates the natural world through acts of faith.

Trust Me because I am trustworthy. I am all-powerful and all-knowing and therefore able to deal with whatever I place on your heart, fully and completely.

Come, let's adventure together in new and wonderful ways.

PROPHETIC ACTS

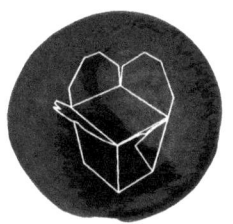

— Take Aways —

God cares more about my obedience and developing my faith than my comfort and ease. Having said that, He knows and loves my personality and won't stretch me beyond my capacity with Him.

Something happens in the natural, which flows into the spiritual and reveals God's intent for that place.

Am I open to the idea of physically acting upon what God shows me to do?

PROPHETIC ACTS ARE SOMETIMES PURELY ABOUT MY OBEDIENCE.

As led by God, amazing things can result from obediently doing what He reveals through prophetic acts.

Some acts have yet to be realised fully, but I wait in trust for breakthrough.

Prophetic acts don't always make much sense at the time, but they do reflect the heart and characteristics of a loving and good Father God.

Sometimes, what I see with my human eyes doesn't measure up with what God is saying. A prophetic act can be about declaring or acting out in faith to agree with God's truth on a matter.

When God prompts an idea in my heart, I 'get to' give it a go. Understanding that God is for me-not against me.

A prophetic act does not go against God's loving and good nature; rather, it aligns with it, and the Word and His fruit of the Spirit.

I might look or feel silly at times, but if I care more about God's opinion of me then the rest won't matter too much.

Faith acts like this can be pride moderators.

PROPHETIC ACTS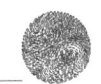

WHAT I SEE, I BEHOLD, AND WHAT I BEHOLD, I CAN BECOME.

When I choose to align myself with God's way, my actions have power. My faith is in the Lord and His ability to act in any given situation.

Prophetic acts can shrink my fear of people, and I have seen and experienced so much breakthrough because of it.

I don't give up because when God prompts, I must follow, knowing it is going to be amazing—full of everything that God is.

What does God see? Does He want me to do an act of faith, agreeing with His vision of how things are, rather than how they look now?

Is there a lack of breakthrough? Does it feel like there is a delay or frustration? It is time to ask God if He wants me to do a prophetic act that might help break through the wall.

CHAPTER SIX

— Questions To Ponder —

1. Was there anything about this area of prophetic acts which stood out to me?

2. What is a prophetic act? Define what it is. What is the purpose of it?

PROPHETIC ACTS

3. What do I personally believe about prophetic acts?

4. What does the Bible say about them? What examples in the Word can I find? What do I observe? What is common and what is different to these examples?

> The Lord said to him, "What is that in your hand?" And he said, "A staff." Then He said, "Throw it on the ground." So he threw it on the ground, and it became a serpent; and Moses fled from it.
>
> EXODUS 4:2-3 NASB95

CHAPTER SIX

5. To what level would I follow a God prompt? Is there anything I'd be unwilling to do if He asked me? (Keeping in mind, that God's instruction will always reflect His heart, the Word of God, and the fruit of His Spirit.)

6. When do I carry out a prophetic act? What calls me to action? How?

> I will stand before you on the rock at Mount Sinai. Strike the rock, and water will come gushing out. Then the people will be able to drink." So Moses struck the rock as he was told, and water gushed out as the elders looked on.
>
> **EXODUS 17:6 NLT**

PROPHETIC ACTS

7. Have I carried out a prophetic act of faith before? Or has someone I've know done one? What did I notice about this? Did it bring a shift, change, or difference?

8. How would I describe what happens spiritually as we partner with God in carrying out a prophetic act? What happens in the natural realm? In the spiritual realm?

> After saying this, he spit on the ground, made some mud with the saliva, and put it on the man's eyes. "Go," he told him, "wash in the Pool of Siloam" (this word means "Sent"). So the man went and washed, and came home seeing.
>
> **JOHN 9:6-7 NIV**

9. What benefits does a willingness to follow His prompting in prophetic acts bring to my person or situation? What could this mean for me now?

> You shall march around the city, all you men of war; you shall go all around the city once. This you shall do six days. And seven priests shall bear seven trumpets of rams' horns before the ark. But the seventh day you shall march around the city seven times, and the priests shall blow the trumpets. It shall come to pass, when they make a long blast with the ram's horn, and when you hear the sound of the trumpet, that all the people shall shout with a great shout; then the wall of the city will fall down flat....
>
> **JOSHUA 6:3-5 NKJV**

PROPHETIC ACTS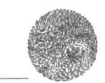

— Playlist —

You Came – Jonathan David & Melissa Helser

On the Shores – Melissa Helser

Oceans – Hillsong United

Holy, Holy, Holy, Lord God Almighty – Reginald Heiber, England (1826)

All I Need Is You – Hillsong United

Come Alive – Hillsong United

It Is Well – Kristine DiMarco

Champion – Maverick City

— Activations —

MUSICAL

Spend some time with God worshipping and seeking His heart.

Specifically ask Him to reveal a situation or person that He wants to broach, if there is something He wants you to do in faith and obedience about what He has revealed. Then do that.

VISUAL

Put on some soaking music and seek God's heart about something you are finding difficult at this time. Ask God how He sees your current hard place and create a visual representation of His version of it. Ask Him for a prophetic act that you can carry out as prompted by Him.

LOGICAL

Explore the many examples of prophetic acts in Scripture.

There are many things that make no human sense, but make perfect sense to God, including praying over hankies (Acts 19:11-12), spitting in mud (John 9:6-7), and anointing with oil (Mark 6:13). What do you notice in these examples? What was required of each person? What was the heart behind it? What was the outcome of these acts of faith? How does this sit with your own faith? Would you be willing to do these same or different things if God prompted you to? Why or why not?

PROPHETIC ACTS

BODILY/KINESTHETIC

Ask God today what He would have you do, then (as long as it aligns with God's loving nature), just do it and watch what happens. Thank Him for what He is doing because He is always active in the world around us.

INTRAPERSONAL

What is your greatest need in your current circumstance?

What is the thickest wall? What is in the way?

Is there a consistent battle or theme in your hard places?

Ask God for clarity about this matter.

Ask Him if He wants you to do anything as a prophetic act of faith and what that is.

LINGUISTIC/VERBAL

Ask God to highlight an area of your life that He wants to touch today.

Ask God how He sees this area of your life.

Take note of the intricacies of what He reveals.

Are there any Scriptures which reflect the heart of what He has shown you?

Now write a prophetic declaration of His heart about the area.

As prompted by Him, meditate on this version regularly.

INTERPERSONAL

Read the passage of Luke 9:16, where Jesus asks the crowd to share a few pieces of bread and fish. And in faith, they are multiplied.

As you read through this passage, ask God what you can do as an act of faith today that would bless someone else or bring breakthrough.

NATURALISTIC

Remember the livestock in the Bible that looked at the marked and speckled sticks in the water, and produced more speckled and marked sheep (Genesis 30:39)?

As you read through this passage, observe your internal response to this miraculous prophetic act.

What do you notice as you read through it?

Consider what/how it can be applied to your own life at this time.

Jesus said to the servants, "Fill the jars with water"; so they filled them to the brim. Then he told them, "Now draw some out and take it to the master of the banquet." They did so, and the master of the banquet tasted the water that had been turned into wine.

JOHN 2:7-9A NIV

CHAPTER SIX

— Bless You —

Bless you, bold, faith-filled one of His.

*I bless you with freedom to trust God as He
reveals creative ways for breakthrough.*

Bless you with fearless faith.

Be blessed as you care more about what God thinks than what others do.

Be blessed with courage to say yes to God, knowing He is trustworthy.

I bless you with confidence that you hear His voice.

*Bless you with knowing what His voice sounds and feels
like, and the wisdom and discernment to follow Him.*

*Be blessed as you experience breakthrough in
your situation as a result of obedience.*

Be blessed as you follow the things of His heart and leading.

*Bless you with clarity and courage to be willing
to step out with Him and adventure.*

Be blessed in the mighty, creative and good name of Jesus,

Amen.

xxxxx

Chapter Seven

JOY

Until now you have not asked for anything
in my name. Ask and you will receive,
and your joy will be complete.

JOHN 16:24 NIV

— Father's Heart —

Joy is My love song to you, My child.

It is a way that I love you with the language of heaven.

Joy is what I use to pour My everything upon you.

It is a door to break through and learn the rhythms of My heartbeat.

Joy is powerful because it is Me, and I want My children to see and experience Me fully.

It is My way for you to experience complete freedom, release, and life!

When circumstances come, endeavouring to take you off the right path, My joy can release everything you need to combat it.

Joy is My gift to you, and it is constantly available to you.

As you step into My rest, you will encounter Me.

My heartbeat never fails to release joy, especially in this space.

Knowing who you are in Me will bring you joy. Joy is present in kingdom identity.

As you know Me more, joy is expanded.

As you learn to trust Me in whatever comes, joy is present.

Joy is a power tool for life that allows you to walk through the tough times and remain centred in Me.

Joy breeds My hope; it's the anchor which holds you steadfast.

The world will tell you, "Strive for happiness!" I say to you, "Strive for more of Me." Then you will have all you need…and more.

As the embers of joy are stoked, it doesn't take much for those tiny sparks to become a wildfire of courage, confidence, and inner delight.

Flames will help to combat the barbs of the enemy, as well as fear, anxiety, worry, and any other negative emotions that come to throw you off your track.

Desire My joy; look for it, reach out for it, and learn to recognise it.

Finding joy in the "Be still" with Me is easier and always available.

Turn your eyes to Me afresh, My beloved. That choice to look up will build your faith as you encounter Me. Know that the more you know Me, the greater you will walk in joy.

My joy supersedes all fear.

Invite Me into every moment, every situation, and ask Me for joy.

Then keep watch! It will not be far away.

JOY

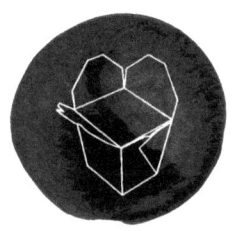

— Take Aways —

Rest in Him; allow Him to show the way back to joy.

As a by-product of the times when I choose to trust God in areas of my life—parenting, marriage, friendship, conflict, family or circumstances—I find I am experiencing joy.

JOY ISN'T HAPPINESS.

Joy can remain despite what comes.

I already have joy, because the wholly joyous and provider God, lives within me, and never leaves me.

Joy is entwined with having hope, and the reason for my hope—Jesus.

Busyness, fear and stress are joy dampeners.

JOY IS INTERNAL AND ALWAYS ACCESSIBLE.

Happiness comes and goes; it's situationally based. Happiness is based on the externals.

Joy is a huge key for breakthrough in difficult circumstances.

Joy is abiding, deeper with Him.

When I am overwhelmed, God reminds me to sing to Him, to dance in my kitchen before Him, and before too long, I recognise His joy in me once again.

JOY

It really shouldn't matter what comes my way because, as challenges occur, they are an opportunity for me to connect with God. This grows our relationship and further reveals His joy in me.

JOY ISN'T BASED ON WHAT IS HAPPENING AROUND ME OR TO ME.

As I am more conscious of Him than anything else, I encounter joy.

As I am at ease with my inner world, this draws a natural joy to me.

I find myself in joy when I am living in the moment, not too far ahead.

I can't be joyful and angry at the same time. Neither can I be joyful and discouraged, joyful and frustrated, joyful and bitter, joyful and fearful or joyful and exhausted. Joy and negative emotions do not seem to combine.

— Questions To Ponder —

1. Was there anything that grabbed my attention about joy?

2. Define joy. What do I believe about joy in life? What is the difference between happiness and joy? Is there a difference? Why or why not?

3. How do I know when I am joyful? What do I feel? How is my internal state? How do I recognise joy?

4. Can I be joyful and heavy in my spirit at the same time? Joyful and fearful? Joyful and angry? Joyful and …? Why or why not?

> Rejoice always, pray continually, give thanks in all circumstances; for this is God's will for you in Christ Jesus.
>
> **1 THESSALONIANS 5:16-18**

5. What does God say about joy? How did Jesus reflect joy? What evidence can I find of this?

6. Thinking of the Trinity, with Whom do I most connect with? Father, Jesus or Holy Spirit? Which part of the Trinity do you most associate with joy? Why? How does connecting with God help me with joy? How do loving parents help their children to foster joy? How does God help me in this same way?

> When anxiety was great within me, your consolation brought me joy.
>
> **PSALM 94:19 NIV**

JOY

7. What are the benefits for joy in my life and circumstance? When joy seems far, far away, what can I do to get back in step with it?

8. Consider this verse: "Be joyful always; pray continually; give thanks in all circumstances for this is God's will for you in Christ Jesus" (1 Thessalonians 5:16 ESV). How is this possible in everyday life? What does it look or feel like? How can joy benefit my current season?

> The hope of the righteous brings joy, but the expectation of the wicked will perish.
>
> **PROVERBS 10:28 ESV**

Although you've never seen him, you love him. Even though you don't see him now, you trust him and so rejoice with a glorious joy that is too much for words.

1 PETER 1:8 CEB

JOY

— Playlist —

Joy of the Lord – Maverick City Music TRIBL

Joyfully – Kari Jobe

Now Unto Him Who Is Able to Keep – Rachel E. Mortishire

At the Cross – Isaac Watts, England (1707)

Marvellous Light – Ellie Holcomb

His Eye Is on the Sparrow – Lauren Hill

Joy – Rend Collective

All Joy No Stress – Rhett Walker

Joy of the Lord – Rend Collective

My Own Little World – Matthew West

— *Activations* —

MUSICAL

Explore or create a piece of music that emits joy! Are there joyful notes? Melodies? Lyrics? What kind of sounds allow joy to bubble up within you? Put a joyous psalm or passage of Scripture to music.

VISUAL

Select the tones and colours that reflect joy to your heart. Now choose a place, a person or a thing that you connect with joy. Put on some music which feels joyous for your internals and create a piece with God that answers the question: "God, what does my joy look like?"

LOGICAL

Consider the Appendix 4 quote from Bill Johnson. What are your thoughts about this and how it relates to joy?

BODILY/KINESTHETIC

Create or build a joy box. Ask God to reveal the things that bring, emit, build, or develop joy in your life. Place reminders of these in your box. As you have need of joy, revisit this box of your joy starters.

JOY

INTRAPERSONAL

Spend some reflective time with God thinking upon the joy timeline of your life. Plot the main events, memories, highs, and lows. Now ask God, "What was joy doing in and around those times?" Write down what you sense Him saying.

LINGUISTIC/VERBAL

Write a personal psalm of joy. Think upon a time in your life where joy was evident. Ask Holy Spirit to remind you of one (if you can't recollect.) Use descriptive language and sensory words that allow your reader to encounter the joy about which you are writing.

INTERPERSONAL

Spend time with a trusted friend or counsellor over a hot cuppa and discuss these verses: "She is clothed with strength and dignity; she can laugh at the days to come." (Proverbs 31:25 NIV) "You have turned my mourning into dancing" (Psalm 30:11a ESV)

NATURALISTIC

In the well-known Christmas carol, "Joy to the World," one of the lyrics states, "And heaven and nature sing." How does nature emit joy in this world? What do you observe in nature that is joyous? In your eyes, how do heaven and nature sing?

— Bless You —

Bless you, one who has joy deep down in their core,

*Be blessed with the revelation that joy never
leaves you—not for a moment.*

Bless you with God's view of joy expressed in your life.

God bless you with increasing joy and freedom in life.

Bless you with a desire to turn to God whenever joy seems absent.

*Be blessed with the kind of internal joy that
bubbles up—even when things are hard.*

*God bless you with an outlook that invites
joy to build, grow, and overflow.*

Bless your body with the full benefits of joy and hope in God.

May your body, soul and spirit be blessed by the One Who is joy itself.

In Jesus' powerful name,

Amen.

xxxxx

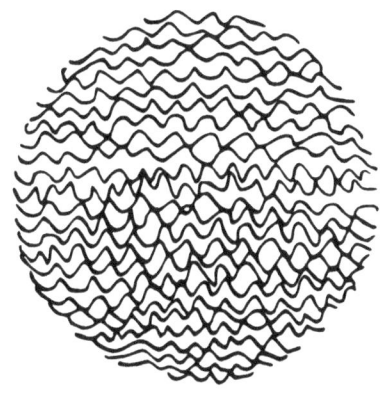

Chapter Eight

INTERCESSION

With all prayer and petition pray at all times in the Spirit and with this in view, be on the alert with all perseverance and petition for all the saints.

EPHESIANS 6:18 NASB 1995

— Father's Heart —

Cry out to Me on behalf of others. Sing to Me of the things that burden you.

Speak to Me and tell Me of the things that bring heaviness to your heart, and I will turn them around.

I will empower you to intercede on behalf of all that you feel, see, and sense from Me.

Trust Me with the things that are too big for words.

Let Me make a heavenly exchange as you hand over troubles for peace and power.

Bring Me the things which take hold of your thoughts, emotions, and heart; start telling Me about them—in whatever way you wish.

Write, speak, dance, sing, draw, or simply allow My Spirit to speak on your behalf.

As you release these things to Me, the realisation of Who I am will be revealed to you in a greater measure.

As you acknowledge Who I am, My great power is released—both in the situation and within you.

You will see My Spirit transform the very things I have placed upon your heart. I allowed these things and hoped you would come and share them with Me, enabling you and those around you to stand in awe of My presence, power, and ability to do immeasurably more than you perceive or hope for.

Have faith; I am always working.

Intercession allows My heartbeat to be felt, displayed, and released by you and the one I placed on your heart.

I allow this so you can see more of Me in the world.

I want you to know and experience Me in all things.

I want you to understand how much you matter to Me.

I want you to catch the heartbeat I have for the world.

I want you to receive a greater understanding and experience of Who I am and the impact I can have in the world through you.

I have allowed certain burdens to impact your heart to build intimacy between us and compassion for others. Encounters like this build your faith.

When you step out and intercede for another, the love I have for you surges through you into the spiritual atmosphere of this world and beyond.

My Spirit loves to flow through these times of togetherness.

When you intercede on behalf of another, it is a step of faith, and I will not disappoint you in it.

I love it when you come, walk, and trust Me with something that might have initially troubled you. As you have trusted and interceded, the weight has released and a heavenly transaction has taken place.

I love to exchange the things of this world for the heavenly things of My kingdom.

Trust Me, My precious, My beloved. "Come to me, all who labor and are heavy laden, and I will give you rest." (Matthew 11:28 ESV). My Word and leading will not return to Me void.

INTERCESSION

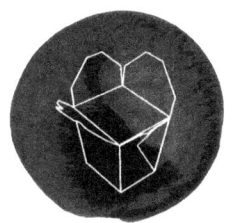

— Take Aways —

Intercession is speaking kingdom principles into earthly failings.

To think that the Creator of all invites me to journey with Him and impact the troubled people and circumstances of this world is too appealing an opportunity to ignore.

INTERCESSION STARTS AND ENDS WITH LOVE.

Intercession is a focused time of choosing to put aside my worries, burdens, and sorrows— and invite another's into my story and pray.

Intercession is praying on behalf of someone or something.

It's a delight in these significant preordained moments to be aligned with God and His heart.

The outcome is not reliant upon me; praying for others is part of God's process and divine plan for village life.

He reveals His heart to willing ones to influence and change things for His children and the world.

Whatever or whoever God shows me to pray for, and if I follow His leading, I can't go wrong.

HE INVITES ME TO PARTNER WITH HIM IN THE MIRACULOUS.

Intercession is an act of obedience to God's call upon our hearts to pray – whether I feel it or not.

It is time to stop when the exchange comes and/or peace lands within me in intercession.

INTERCESSION

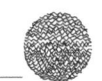

Does God need me to pray for things to shift? God is all powerful, and I am certain that He doesn't need me to pray in order to shift something, but I know it is an invitation to partner with Him.

GOD BLESSES THE TIME WE RELEASE TO HIM.

What my human eyes see is not what God sees, and God is always doing something.

Prayerful intercession reflects aspects of God's nature.

It's a privilege to speak life words, to be a part of something that is bigger than me, and to watch what God unfolds.

It brings God's heart for His children to us because He loves us.

Intercession can change others' circumstances, and in doing so, God has also lifted and I am blessed in the process. I do not intercede so I can be blessed, but it is part of God's miraculous ways. (Psalm 30:11, John 14:27, Ephesians 2:4-5).

— Questions to Ponder —

1. Was there anything about intercession that jumped out to me?

2. Define intercession. Who is it for? What is its purpose?

INTERCESSION

3. How has intercession impacted my life in the past/today? How important is intercession to me on a scale of 1 to 10? (1—of no importance, 10—of greatest importance)

4. Are there any stumbling blocks for me to intercede on behalf on another person or situation? If so, what? Ask God about these. Does interceding cost me? If so, how? Is it worth it?

> First of all, then, I urge that entreaties and prayers, petitions and thanksgivings, be made on behalf of all men.
>
> 1 TIMOTHY 2:1 NASB 95

CHAPTER EIGHT

5. What does the Bible tell me about intercession?

6. Why intercede at all? If I don't feel compelled to intercede, should I still do it? How do I know when to pray for others? What are the things that alert me to begin praying?

> Because I know this will lead to my deliverance through your prayers and help from the Spirit of Jesus Christ.
>
> **PHILIPPIANS 1:19 HCSB**

INTERCESSION

7. How is intercession a large part of the Christian faith? How does it relate to being a part of the body of Christ? What would the world/church look like without intercession? What might life look like if all Jesus followers interceded as prompted by Him?

8. Jesus intercedes on behalf of me to the Father (Romans 8:34). What would life look like if I asked Jesus what He is interceding for, before the Father and prayed that?

> Seek the welfare of the city where I have sent you into exile and pray to the Lord on its behalf; for in its welfare you will have welfare.
>
> **JEREMIAH 29:7 NASB 95**

9. What benefits does intercession bring to the lives of others? To my life? What advantages could intercession bring to my own hard seasons?

10. How do I see God's fingerprint in the theme of intercession? What can I see as His greater purpose through it?

Pray in the Spirit at all times and on every occasion. Stay alert and be persistent in your prayers for all believers everywhere.

EPHESIANS 6:18 NIV

INTERCESSION

11. Please rate the importance of intercession again from 1 to 10. Ask God to reveal my next step. It can begin as simply as asking, "Jesus, who are You praying for now that you want me to pray for?" Start somewhere and leap in, knowing that this investment is greater than I'll ever know.

> I urge, then, first of all, that petitions, prayers, intercession and thanksgiving be made for all people—for kings and all those in authority, that we may live peaceful and quiet lives in all godliness and holiness.
>
> **1 TIMOTHY 2:1-2 NIV**

In the same way, the Spirit helps us in our weakness. We do not know what we ought to pray for, but the Spirit himself intercedes for us through wordless groans.

ROMANS 8:26 NIV

INTERCESSION

Playlist

First – Lauren Daigle

I Can Only Imagine – Mercy Me

Gracefully Broken – Tasha Cobbs Leonard

Find Your Wings – Mark Harris

Build Your Kingdom Here – Rend Collective

The Words I Would Say – Sidewalk Prophets

As I Lay Me Down – Sophie B. Hawkins

CHAPTER EIGHT

— Activations —

MUSICAL

Ask Holy Spirit to highlight someone or something
He wants you to intercede on behalf of.

Ask what He wants you to pray—then using instrument or voice, spend time pressing in for who or what He shows you. Keep going until you sense an exchange has been made.

VISUAL

Ask Holy Spirit to put someone on your heart. Ask Jesus what He is interceding on their behalf. Ask Him for a picture of what answered prayer looks like. Create what He revealed to you. If He gives you the green light, share this with the person to give them hope. If it isn't for sharing, pray for them, declaring what He had you create.

LOGICAL

Spend some time in the Word, finding biblical examples of intercession. What do you observe? What benefits are there? How do we intercede? How can you apply what you've learnt to everyday life? Ask God how He wants you to engage with intercession.

INTERCESSION

BODILY/KINESTHETIC

Create a dance or a string of movements that tell a story about a time in your life when others interceded on your behalf, and you experienced breakthrough as a result of their faithfulness.

If you haven't experienced this, ask God how you can intercede for someone at this time using movement.

INTRAPERSONAL

What do you most need prayer for at the moment? Where are you in need of a breakthrough? Where do you need God's touch in your life? Ask Jesus what He is interceding on your behalf. Ask for a picture of what He is praying. If prompted, ask a trusted friend/group to intercede on your behalf.

LINGUISTIC/VERBAL

Write a prayer of intercession on behalf of someone. Instead of focusing upon the problem or the battle, ask Jesus what He is praying—and pray that with the written word. As you write with Him, take note of any exchange in language, emotion, or sense of peace. Ask God what He wants you to do with this written prayer intercession.

INTERPERSONAL

Spend some quality time praying with a friend. Let this be a time of pressing in, and agreement with one another for who or what God is placing upon your heart. Note down any impressions or leadings that He gives to either of you. Remember to celebrate and thank God for all He brings.

NATURALISTIC

Consider Luke 19:40. What does this verse reveal about the passion behind God's heart and His plans coming to fruition? Could this be applied to the area of intercession? (If human beings won't pray, then He'll make nature cry out in unison for the things of His heart.) Research other biblical passages of flora and fauna crying out, speaking, expressing the things of God's heart. How can this be applied to your life?

He was amazed to see that no
one intervened to help the oppressed.
So he himself stepped in to save them with his
strong arm, and his justice sustained him.

ISAIAH 59:16 NLT

— Bless You —

Bless you, one who is an integral part of something much bigger than yourself.

Bless you with encountering the blessing of being interceded for by others.

Be blessed in hearing Jesus' intercession on your behalf.

Bless you with an awareness and care for others as He draws them to your heart and mind.

God bless you with knowing that you are valued and of such great worth that your life is not just your own, but you are a part of the whole body.

Be blessed as you choose to intercede for another who might never know but will be impacted by your prayers of faith.

Bless you with freedom and blessing as you invest time in your day to bless someone else.

God bless you with sensing His leading as you bring all sorts of prayers to Him on behalf of others.

I bless you with encountering the fun it can be to engage with Him in this way.

Bless you with deep, abiding peace as He hears every utterance from your lips and answers each one.

Bless you with seeing breakthroughs, miracles, the signs, and wonders of God as you pray.

Be blessed with greater blessing in your life as a result of intercession.

In Jesus' name,

Amen.

xxxxx

Chapter Nine

LOOKING BEYOND MYSELF

The generous will prosper; those who refresh others will themselves be refreshed.

PROVERBS 11:25 NLT

— Father's Heart —

Life is a gift not meant to be about you alone, My child, but not because you aren't important.

Rather, I know how much you flourish when in community with others.

I designed you this way, and it's a beautiful thing.

Your heart is wired with perfect intricacy for village life.

Are you heavy-hearted, weary, or tired of the depths you now walk?

One of the things that can help is peeking outside your own walls.

Look up and beyond the seemingly constant pressure or your current season.

This is no mere mistake; I created you for kinship with others—each pouring into one another in healthy, selfless loving acts of kindness.

One lifts another, and when that one is lowly, I bring another to lift them!

Even if no one is willing, I will show up Myself for them!

I invite you into this place of giving and receiving as led by My heart. Do you want adventure? More in life? To feel as though you are not alone in all you do?

Time to connect! Time to rise above your situation and pour.

Don't worry. You won't be doing this from your resource and energy alone, I will provide all you need. Lo and behold, you'll find yourself with over and above what you give out.

My currency makes no human sense, and this makes Me laugh out loud at times as you realise I do not work as the world works.

I did not create you only to look inside but to the needs of those around you. I created you to be communal and relational, My child.

When you find yourself only focusing on the things happening within and to you, then you often feel far from Me.

Circumstances will look to distract you from what I want for you.

They will try and take your eyes from Me and on to the things that bring you down, loading heavy weights upon you, obscuring hope.

Life can feel harder than it needs to be in this place.

My words and ways are the ones that will bring life. They will encourage, lighten, and brighten your days, as well as the lives of those around you.

It brings Me great joy when My children choose to look out for one another—when they love one another out of My strength and abundance.

My loving plans long to lift your eyes from what you see, feel, or humanly know—moving them towards Me. As your focus shifts, you see beyond your current circumstance. It's often out of your weakness where I can work with you to invest in and bring life to someone else. This brings so much to others but also to you as you exchange heaviness for hope.

This idea of exchange is not a new concept but one that reveals My very heartbeat to you—if you'll choose to say, "Yes!"

If you are in a lowly place, ask Me to highlight someone for you. As you pray, I will lift and bring life to both of you.

LOOKING BEYOND MYSELF

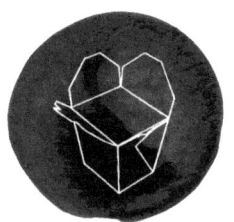

— *Take Aways* —

Each weakness is an opportunity to connect with Holy Spirit, and then to choose to step forward as He prompts. He will fill the gap between what I am and what He is calling me to do.

There are times and seasons for everything, there is a time to receive and be tended to—but not all the time.

IF HE LEADS ME, HE ALSO RESOURCES ME FOR ACTION.

I'd prefer to adventure with God than to sit and ponder how much pain I am in or how much I've lost.

Problems are a constant, but so are His plans to turn them about.

At the very least looking outside of myself has potentially helped someone else. At the most, it has acted as a circuit breaker for my own problems.

The 'random' God moments have brought me more life than what I've endeavoured to walk out by myself.

It is easy for my own problems to become bigger when they are all I focus on.

The very thing that might bring some breakthrough is the thing I feel least like doing—helping another person.

WHEN I CHOOSE TO LOOK OUTSIDE MYSELF, MY FOCUS IS SHIFTED FROM ME TO HE.

Following God's leading in loving others is always the right decision.

LOOKING BEYOND MYSELF

When the weight of circumstances have seemed insurmountable, I've not been able to think of much else. Many times, God has gently directed me to look outside of myself.

OPPORTUNITIES OPEN UP AS PART OF GOD'S GREAT STORY FOR MANKIND.

Share, give, connect, create, encourage, lift, love—follow His prompts, and He will bless my obedience.

If I have breath, I have purpose and something of value to bring to others.

Looking outside of myself is unselfish, but it can also help to reframe my current personal situation.

Are you noticing wonderful things or naturally "knowing" things about others that are good? Take time to listen; God is speaking! Ask, "What do You want me to do with what You are telling me, Lord?"

— Questions To Ponder —

1. Were there any thoughts or prompts that jumped out in this chapter?

2. What do I believe is at the heart of looking outside of myself?

3. How was I raised? Was this concept a part of what was taught to me? Why or why not?

4. What have I observed—both positive and negative—in how others look to their own needs and the needs of others? Is one better than another? If I had a picture of a seesaw with my needs at one end and the needs of others at the other end, where would I sit? What does this reveal about me in this season?

So, encourage each other and build each other up, just as you are already doing.

1 THESSALONIANS 5:11

CHAPTER NINE

5. What has my experience taught me about looking to the needs of others? What are some of the traps and pitfalls I need to be aware of at either end of the seesaw?

6. What disadvantages are there when I only look to the needs of others? What disadvantages are there when I only look to my needs and problems? What can be at the root of this kinds of belief? (Consider an orphan spirit, rejection, performance mentality, people pleasing, etc.)

> Let each of you look not only to his own interests, but also to the interests of others.
>
> **PHILIPPIANS 2:4 ESV**

7. Are there any stumbling blocks I currently have with looking to the needs of others and following God prompts to help? Talk to God about these.

8. What do I believe is God's ideal when it comes to looking to the needs of others and my own needs? Why? What evidence do I have for this belief?

And do not forget to do good and to share with others, for with such sacrifices God is pleased.

HEBREWS 13:16 NIV

CHAPTER NINE

9. What does the Bible tell me about others and their needs? How did Jesus navigate this? Ask Holy Spirit to bring a specific passage to mind.

10. When I step away from my own depths and look outside of ourselves, what benefits have I experienced or noticed in others? How could this benefit me in hard seasons?

> Kind words are like honey,
> sweet to the soul and
> healthy for the body.
>
> **PROVERBS 16:24 NLT**

LOOKING BEYOND MYSELF

—Playlist—

Purify My Heart – Jeremy Riddle/Vineyard Anaheim Worship Moment

Just Say Jesus – 7eventh Time Down

With Every Act of Love – Jason Gray

The Proof of Your Love – For King and Country

Here I Am Send Me – Darlene Zschech

City On Our Knees – TobyMac

Nothing Else – Cody Carnes

Thank You Jesus for the Blood – Charity Gayle

— Activations —

MUSICAL

Spend some time in worship. Breathe with Him. Now ask Him for someone who needs some encouragement today. Send that person whatever has most impacted your heart in this time.

VISUAL

Ask God to highlight someone who is worse off than you are in this current season. Ask Him what would bless them and lift them up. Create with "Father's heart" as your inspiration.

LOGICAL

Write down the benefits of putting your own circumstances to the side and looking to the needs of others. Research these benefits. What biblical examples can you find of this? How can these be applied to your situation today?

BODILY/KINESTHETIC

Ask God to highlight who needs a hug—either physical or metaphorical. Then do that. Take note of what happens to your own heavies as you love others.

INTRAPERSONAL

Consider how looking to the needs of others might add value to your current circumstance. Think upon your unique design and what kinds of things you've noticed about giving to others when walking through your own tough time. What gems can you carry forward into future situations from this?

LINGUISTIC/VERBAL

Ask God to reveal someone who needs some words of encouragement. Now write a life declaration of blessing for this person with Him. Gift it to him or her.

INTERPERSONAL

Read and discuss the parable of the talents with a trusted friend (Matthew 25:14-30). No matter how little we feel we have in our hands in this moment, how will we use it, invest, or spend it? Are you willing to open your hands, lift them to the Father, and say, "I have so little to give right now, Lord, but if I can do anything for You, please help my eyes, heart, and palms to remain open and willing to follow whatever You put before me."

Make plans with a friend to do something practical for someone who is in need as led by Him.

NATURALISTIC

Collect some cuttings or create a bouquet using those things to which God draws your eye. Gift it to someone who needs a bit of tender loving care.

— Bless You —

Bless you, one who is led by the Father's heart in life.

*Be blessed with health, resources, and freedom
to follow His flow and leading.*

God bless you with a divine balance in boundaries and selflessness.

Be blessed with a desire to love others—even when it's hard.

*Bless you with an outpouring of energy and resource
to bless those He brings along your path.*

*Bless your life with a desire to connect with Father
and follow His heart in all things.*

Be blessed with open communication and sharing between you and God.

*God bless you with promptings, energy, time, and
resource to adventure with Him.*

Bless you with 1 Corinthians 13 love in your life.

In Jesus' name,

Amen.

XXXXX

Chapter Ten

SOUND TEACHING

*For I give you sound teaching;
do not abandon my instruction.*

PROVERBS 4:2 NASB

— Father's Heart —

I have placed before you an abundance of food—teaching that would feed the entire world for thousands of years.

I partner with My children to speak life into your situation through this rich feast.

Walk alongside Me and ask Me where to begin.

I will place the keys in your palm; all you need to do is put the key in the lock and turn.

Do you need clarity and peace?

Do you need next steps and instruction?

Do you need hope in your current season?

Are you lacking something but don't know what?

Get back to My foundations; My solid teaching is good for your health, body, soul, and mind.

Sound teaching helps create a good foundation for Me to build upon.

Feed on the things of My heart, and you'll find yourself never wanting.

The world has so much to offer, and at times, it can be overwhelming.

I gently take your hand and lead you to the things that count. Those teachings which will speak right to the heart of the matter.

I long for you to grasp My heartbeat and My love for you.

My Spirit will guide you to the best teaching for your circumstance, helping you to step out in My freedom once more.

There is a smorgasbord of teaching before you, and this can be overwhelming. As you are walk closely with Me, you will become familiar with My wisdom, truth, and prompting to know what is best.

I will protect your heart from that which is not of Me.

I will allow the things that your body, mind, soul, emotions and spirit need to soak in as you consume heartily.

A message inspired by Me, applied and adopted, can change your circumstance and the world around you.

My inspired teaching draws the heart toward Me. I speak with authority, truth and always with love at its core.

Take, eat of the good food I have placed before you. Then go into the world I have placed you and let My words move and empower you to do good works, speak life, and to walk in My freedom.

Do this that others may see and acknowledge Me, that they will turn and thank Me for you and the things you have done in My name.

SOUND TEACHING

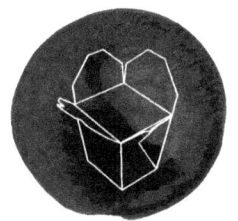

— *Take Aways* —

Much teaching is available to me in this age and a variance of truth within it. I am warned in the Word to keep watch over what teachings I choose to embrace (and with good reason).

Thankfully, God's Word and its principles are unchanging and continue to be as relevant today as they were 2000 years ago.

SOLID TEACHING = GOOD HEALTHY FOOD.

What I consume can influence my thoughts, feelings, behaviours.

If I surround myself with teaching that is human opinion alone, my hope levels can drop.

If I surround myself with sound biblical and Holy-Spirit-inspired teaching, my entire being can soar.

Sound teaching refers to foundational truths of God's heart for me, and for others.

There is much that can lead me down paths I was not designed for and will not benefit me in this season.

SOUND TEACHING IS THE BACKBONE OF SPIRITUAL GROWTH.

God brings teaching alongside me at exactly the right times with answers to the questions I have been wrestling with.

SOUND TEACHING

Asking God for His discernment and wisdom for the right teaching at the right time is always a good idea.

TAKE THE TIME TO NOTE WHAT I AM LISTENING TO AND WATCHING IN TERMS OF TEACHING.

Anointed teaching can heal, refresh, and align me with God's heartbeat.

I am always consuming something. What will I feast on today?

If I don't keep watch for what I am consuming, it can consume me.

Placing God above all pastors, teachers and preachers will help me not to create idols out of people. God can show the way, revealing what teaching He wants me to watch or listen to in this season.

— *Questions To Ponder* —

1. Are there things in this area of foundational teaching that leap out to me?

2. Has teaching changed over time? How? Why?

SOUND TEACHING

3. What foundational, solid, sound teaching over the years has impacted my heart for the good?

4. Have there been times where teaching has been sound, but teachers have not been? How do I come to peace about this matter? What does God say about it?

> So Jesus answered them and said, "My teaching is not mine, but His who sent me."
>
> **JOHN 7:16 NASB1995**

5. What beliefs do I hold about teaching and teachers? Where have these come from? Do they align with God's heart? Have I ever placed Bible preachers on a pedestal? Ask God more about this.

6. Are there any roadblocks to me surrounding myself with healthy, God-inspired teaching?

> Holding fast the faithful word which is in accordance with the teaching, so that he will be able to both exhort in sound doctrine and to refute those who contradict.
>
> **TITUS 1:9 NASB1995**

7. What benefits could feasting on sound teaching bring me in this season? How might it affect my life and perspectives? How could it impact my health and relationships? What will it do for God and my relationship?

8. How will I know when something is sound? What will be my yardstick? How will I measure internally whether or not something is good for me? What will I do if I find something isn't healthy? What indicators will alert me to this fact?

Retain the standard of sound words which you have heard from me, in the faith and love which are in Christ Jesus.

2 TIMOTHY 1:13

9. What do I currently consume in life? Where is my time invested? How am I blessing my body, soul, and mind? How does sound teaching fit? Is it where I want it to be? Ask God more about these things.

> In pointing out these things to the brethren, you will be a good servant of Christ Jesus, constantly nourished on the words of the faith and of the sound doctrine which you have been following.
>
> **1 TIMOTHY 4:6 NASB1995**

SOUND TEACHING

—Playlist—

Refiner's Fire – Brian Doerksen

What a Beautiful Name – Hillsong Worship

Hallelujah (Friend and King) – Tim Hughes

God So Loved – We the Kingdom

Isaiah Song – Maverick City TRBL

Mount Zion – Jonathan Helser & Cageless Birds (live at home version)

Psalm 23 – (Bible Study Tools & Videos, YouTube version)

— Activations —

MUSICAL

Research and source some worship music that is purely based on sound teaching. Or better still, create lyrics or a piece of music that reflects a recent truth that He revealed through sound teaching.

VISUAL

Can you recall the last time you heard a solid impacting message? Ask Holy Spirit to remind you of this time or of truths He has brought through sound teaching. Now represent this moment, teaching or feeling in an art form. Produce something or be freshly inspired as you reflect upon the benefits of grounding our faith in solid teaching.

LOGICAL

What are some of the solid teachings of faith with God through Jesus? What are the deal breakers? What theology is non-negotiable if you are walking with Him? Consider how this might draw the church together if we focused upon these. What would be the benefits and/or disadvantages of walking together this way. How can you apply this to your life today?

SOUND TEACHING

BODILY/KINESTHETIC

Athletes train regularly using tried and tested methods to bring out the greatest performance. How can this be applied in the area of sound teaching? What steps can you take to either increase or begin feeding on this in your life? What benefits to your spiritual training might this bring?

INTRAPERSONAL

Think upon those times where the rough weather of life has tried to toss you about (James 1:2-18). Spend some time resting with Holy Spirit, asking God to reveal what He wants you to know in this season of life. Consider some foundational areas of teaching that don't change over time.

LINGUISTIC/VERBAL

Consider the idea of timeless truths.

Write a piece that reveals the benefits of investing in the things that provide solid foundation in faith. Have you walked through a time where sound teaching has been an anchor for your heart? Write from this point of view.

INTERPERSONAL

Connect with a friend to study some good, solid teaching—timeless teaching that remains unchanged despite the era in which we live. Discuss, encourage and cheer each other on in this area. Ask one another how this teaching can be applied to everyday life. Keep it practical. Sound teaching can always be applied or adopted.

NATURALISTIC

Make the decision to listen to some sound teaching when out in nature. As you listen, walk with God in it. Observe what He reveals to you through your senses in the natural environment.

Anyone who goes too far and does not abide in the teaching of Christ, does not have God; the one who abides in the teaching, he has both the Father and the Son.

2 JOHN 1:9 NASB1995

SOUND TEACHING

— Bless You —

Bless you, one who has access to so much that is good and healthy in life.

God bless you with a desire to know Him more.

Bless you with an appreciation of the feast of teaching available for you at this time.

Be blessed with godly discernment in knowing when to draw near and when to step back from certain teachings.

Bless you with encountering His heart for your specific season through solid teaching.

Be blessed with a faith that goes from strength to strength with Him.

Be blessed with a passion for His Word, His heart, and His adventures in your life.

Bless you with wisdom to draw near to Him, attuning to His leading.

Bless your heart with protection from anything that isn't from Him and a heart that is wired for His truth.

Be blessed with His antennae of truth and love in your life.

In Jesus' name,

Amen.

xxxxx

Chapter Eleven

THE WORD

Your word is a lamp for my feet, a light on my path.

PSALM 119:105 NIV

— Father's Heart —

My Word is My bond.

My promise to you is that you are never alone.

It holds every promise I give to you for life and the lives of those around you.

It holds the ultimate story of hope and forgiveness.

It gives you a reason and purpose.

I set out My guidelines to live well and full of joy.

I have created you to be a part of My Word and an integral part of My story.

You have a choice, My child, to be a part of, or apart from My story.

I will not force this upon you.

Rest before Me and ask Me to show you where to begin.

Then read and rest, read and rest, read and rest.

Keep reading until my Spirit highlights a word or a passage. This is where you are to stop and let it soak in.

Ask My Holy Spirit to reveal the truth of what you are reading.

Ask Me how it relates to you.

*Reading without rest can feel lifeless and without
power: You've tried that many times before.*

*Come experience My rest; in this, My presence
will make the Word come alive in you.*

It is always living, but you need to be alive in it!

*When this happens, My Word will jump off
the page and encourage you greatly!*

Feed yourself, My child, by being in My word.

I wrote My love letter just for you.

I give you every reason to know that you are loved and valued by Me.

I know you so well, My child, and I want the best for you.

Come to Me and My word often. I will speak to you. I will encourage you.

I will instruct you to eat buffets of richness before your enemies!

My word will guide you, speak to you, and uplift you.

I will tell you what to do and when.

*As you learn to trust, ask Me questions and then where to find
answers in My Word. There is nothing that is absent from
My heart, and the Word is inspired by that. My Spirit will
prompt you with answers or guide you where to begin.*

*Explore my Word, dwell in it, let it infiltrate your heart,
and the very best of Me will shine through you*

THE WORD

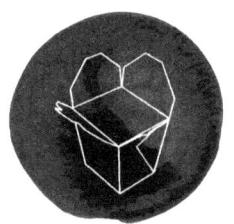

— Take Aways —

Apps, devotionals, worship music, podcasts, newsletters, various translations, audiobooks… the sky's the limit. Draw near to Him through His Word, and life will be better.

Reading the Word is relational—not a task to be checked off the list.

I AM LIVING SCRIPTURE IN HIS EYES.

Reading the Word for the season I am in is, priceless.

Even when I don't feel it, it is still imparting something.

- Do I need help? Study the theme of the solution to my problem.

- Do I want activation and inspiration? Check out the miracles of Jesus.

- If I never connect with God or His Word, then I soon find I haven't met with Him in a while.

- If I read until I feel something land or jump out, that is often Holy Spirit revealing something. Start a conversation with Him about it.

HIS WORD IS A SPRINGBOARD FOR EVERYTHING GOOD IN LIFE.

- As I highlight verses, commonalities, and make notes, I realise that God speaks powerfully to me through His incredible Word.

THE WORD

The Bible is NOT a dead document, but a living one! Start opening up communication with Him through His Word. God never disappoints!

A SINGLE VERSE CAN CHANGE A DAY OR A LIFETIME!

Am I wanting clarity and direction? Greater wisdom and discernment? Check out Proverbs and the prophets.

The Bible isn't an outdated book, but a living organism of life.

Whatever the theme—direction, connection, enfolding, love, identity, strategies, inspiration, collection, community, faith, building hope, purpose, meaning and soooooo much more—it is found in the Word.

— Questions To Ponder —

1. What stood out to me about the Word in this chapter?

2. What do I believe about the Bible? Where did it come from? What is true about it? Reflect on the Bible and God's part in it.

THE WORD

3. What have I been taught to do with the Bible? Has this changed over the years?

4. How do I feel about the Bible? Reading the Bible? Do I find it easy or hard? What helps me dive into the Word?

> He replied, "Blessed rather are those who hear the word of God and obey it."
>
> **LUKE 11:28 NIV**

5. How have I interacted with the Word in my life? When have I experienced or heard from God through it? What happened?

6. What do I desire at my core regarding the Bible? How do I see its role in my faith?

> For the word of the Lord is right and true; he is faithful in all he does.
>
> **PSALM 33:4 NIV**

7. Are there any stumbling blocks to my getting into the Word? What are these? What does God say to me about this? Is there a way forward to make it more my style of ingesting? Ask Holy Spirit to reveal pointers for this.

8. What is my response when reading this quote: "Learning to love the Word is learning to love the One it is about." Do I agree or disagree? Why?

In the beginning was the word, and the word was with God, and the word was God.

JOHN 1:1 NIV

9. What benefits might there be to my faith if I prioritised time with God and His Word?

> For the word of God is alive and active. Sharper than any double-edged sword, it penetrates even to dividing soul and spirit, joints and marrow; it judges the thoughts and the attitudes of the heart.
>
> **HEBREWS 4:12 NIV**

THE WORD

—Playlist—

Agnus Dei – Michael W Smith

Ancient Words – Robin Mark

How Great Thou Art – Carl Gustav Boberg, Sweden (1885)

Thy Word – Amy Grant

Word of God Speak – Mercy Me

Yes and Amen – Housefires

Turn Your Eyes Upon Jesus – Lauren Daigle

Zion – Aaron Shust

Your Word – Awakening Music

CHAPTER ELEVEN

— *Activations* —

MUSICAL

Research the musical passages in the Bible and select one for this activation. Read it across the various translations. Take a moment to sit with Him in the silence. Listen to what He is saying. Ask Him for a way to put what He has shared to music/song.

VISUAL

Ask Holy Spirit what God's Word is like or check out Appendix 5. Read the story of the scuba diver Holy Spirit gave. Represent either image. Let this be a message artwork.

Create a promise artwork. Research the language and Hebrew/Greek meaning of each word of the verse. Now represent this with His flow being your source of inspiration.

LOGICAL

Ask God to lead you to a passage of Scripture or verse that is for your current season. Spend some time pulling apart this Scripture, studying each word. Look into the context and meaning. Ask God for His interpretation. As an add on, consider reading what others have gleaned from this same biblical reference.

THE WORD

BODILY/KINESTHETIC

Using only your hands, create something that reflects a Bible promise that speaks to and encourages your heart—whatever the season. Write out one of your "life" Bible verses in sand or soil.

INTRAPERSONAL

Consider any areas where your faith feels a little stale, challenged, or in need of some refreshing. Ask God to highlight a story, a passage, or a verse that speaks to this.

LINGUISTIC/VERBAL

Spend some time researching and then producing a piece of writing that speaks to a relevant theme in your current season. Look up every verse based on this theme and let them marinate in your heart. Note down the things that jump out or that you find encouraging, interesting or tug at your heart. Ask God what to do with this today.

INTERPERSONAL

Make a commitment with a friend to keep one another accountable in reading the Word. Check in regularly and share insights, spurring one another on in the study of the Word. Focus on quality, rather than quantity—as it isn't a task, but rather a relational journey with Him.

NATURALISTIC

Spend some time in nature looking into what the Bible says about creation. As phrases and words comes to mind, look them up. Are you noticing leaves? Look up where the Word talks about leaves. Are you noticing clouds or sky? Look up these verses. Note down what He shows you about these. God is speaking to you through Creation and His Word.

— Bless You —

Be blessed, one who is loved by the inspiration of the Word.

Bless you with a heart to know Him to a greater measure in every way.

Be blessed with reading His Word with fresh eyes.

Bless you with a heart-to-heart connection with the Bible and its truths.

Bless you with fresh revelation, today's manna, through the Word.

*Be blessed, cherished one, as He reveals His
great love for you through Jesus.*

God bless you with a heart that daily devours His Words of life.

Bless you with the Bible coming alive for you today!

In Jesus' name,

Amen.

xxxxx

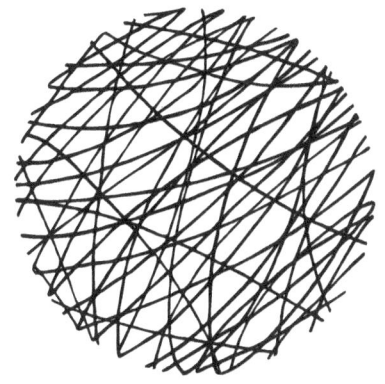

Chapter Twelve

VISIONS

And the Spirit lifted me up and brought me in a vision by the Spirit of God to the exiles in Chaldea. So the vision that I had seen left me. Then I told the exiles all the things that the Lord had shown me.

EZEKIEL 11:24-25 NASB1995

— Father's Heart —

I have created you to see things.

As you connect with and trust Me, I will show you great and inexplicable things. I long to show you more, but you are not quite ready for that, My child. I will only reveal what you are ready to receive, and what I give you will be good.

Come and trust Me to show and tell you whatever you need for that moment and beyond.

I give visions for specific purposes.

I use them as keys to speak to and show you something you need to see. I love to reveal amazing things to you because it shares another part of Myself with you.

Trust Me with whatever I wish to show you.

Be open to new opportunities, My child. I rarely do two things the same way.

Things you could not even imagine. As you know Me, you can trust Me, child. I will not lead you astray.

Test the things that you receive, and if they do not fit with My nature and Word, let them go.

*If they do align then embrace them. I will show
you wonderful truths through them.*

*Do not be disappointed about how I show
myself to you or how I speak to you.*

*I know you best, and I know at times you have desired
something other than what I am giving you.*

*Trust Me with how I reveal Myself, and you
will be in the safest hands—Mine.*

I love you dearly, My precious child; there is much adventure ahead.

Hang on to Me tightly, and we can enjoy the ride together.

VISIONS

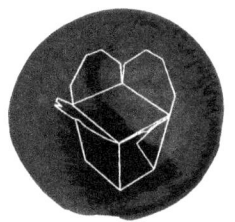

— *Take Aways* —

Part of getting to know God as a loving Father means His gifts are a by-product of this connection. Sometimes this will come in creative forms.

Visions can reveal what has happened but also what is to come. They can be empowering, encouraging, and timely.

Visions have since been explained to me as being a picture or a scene from God that can be seen with open eyes.

Visions are just one way God can communicate with us.

Visions are God pictures that can be seen with the human and my mind's eye.

Visions are a God-given gift—not something that is earnt or humanly strived for.

Visions are mentioned many times in the Bible, and I believe are for today.

Visions often are God's revealing something to me.

Visions get my attention.

My motivation is always best when I seek to know God more rather than His gifts.

Not unlike dreams, God can use visions to encourage, teach, challenge, or to love.

VISIONS

My experience of visions is that they are real pictures or moving scenes that can be explored.

TO DESIRE GOD IS THE BEST GIFT OF ALL.

Commonly we are awake with visions and asleep with dreams.

Visions often feel so real that I can reach out and touch it (and I've tried).

I have had visions that I can see with my eyes open or closed.

Visions are one of the ways God has spoken in this season of suffering. They have been a key He has used, not only to survive hardship, but to thrive within it.

CHAPTER TWELVE

— Questions to Ponder —

1. What leapt out to me from this chapter?

2. What do I believe about God-given visions? Are they for now? Why or why not?

VISIONS

3. What makes something a vision? What elements?

4. Have I ever been given a vision from God? Do I know of anyone who has? What did it reveal about God?

While the food was being prepared, he fell sound asleep and had a vision.

ACTS 10:10B CEV

5. Am I open to receiving a vision from God? What internal response does it create in me? Fear, trepidation, excitement? Why? Do I desire to receive visions from God? Why or why not?

6. What does the Bible reveal about the nature of God-given visions?

> And he said, "Hear my words: If there is a prophet among you, I the Lord make myself known to him in a vision; I speak with him in a dream.
>
> **NUMBERS 12:6 ESV**

7. What do I believe is God's intention in giving a vision? Why?

8. Have I ever desired God's benefits more than simply desiring Him? How can I keep my motives pure? How does God view this? What does God desire from me?

> One afternoon about three o'clock, he had a vision in which he saw an angel of God coming toward him. "Cornelius!" the angel said.
>
> **ACTS 10:3 NLT**

9. Write an unfiltered, honest prayer to God about your willingness to receive the gifts He has for me.

> Boasting is necessary, though it is not profitable; but I will go on to visions and revelations of the Lord. I know a man in Christ who fourteen years ago—whether in the body I do not know, or out of the body I do not know, God knows—such a man was caught up to the third heaven.
>
> **2 CORINTHIANS 12:1-2 NASB1995**

VISIONS

Playlist

How He Loves – Crowder

Open Heaven – Hillsong Worship

There Is a Cloud – Elevation Worship

God of Wonders – Third Day

This Is a Move – Brandon Lake, Bethel Music

Believe for It – CeCe Winans

Gifts from God – Chris Tomlin

— Activations —

A vision is a gift from God—not something that is strived for or earnt. These activations endeavour to connect you to a greater depth to Father and His heart of love for you and to learn more about visions.

MUSICAL

Reflect upon Joel 2:28. Using your instrument of choice, spend time creating the sound of Holy Spirit pouring out His Spirit upon all.

VISUAL

Select one biblical vision and spend some time pondering this event. Ask Holy Spirit for His insight and revelation about it. What does He reveal? What is He saying to you about it? Now express this artistically.

LOGICAL

Study the difference between dreams and visions. What biblical evidence can you find of God-given visions. What do you observe from what you've read? Ask Holy Spirit for His insight. What are the outcomes and purposes when people received a vision?

BODILY/KINESTHETIC

Spend some quiet time with God, meditating on His nature, resting before Him. Let your body be still at this time. Become aware of all the inner workings of your body and its systems—let them quieten before Him as you are still. In the stillness, take time to simply listen. Let His heart speak to yours.

INTRAPERSONAL

What is your personal motivation to connect with God? Is it wholly selfless? Being honest with yourself, what is it that you want from God? Why do you connect with Him?

LINGUISTIC/VERBAL

Select a biblical example of a God-given vision. Imagine yourself as the main character in the event. Step inside their skin and write from their point of view; share the event with a friend through your words. Breathe life into the story through the use of your senses and language.

INTERPERSONAL

Spend some time with a trusted prayer counsellor, friend, or Holy Spirit. Take time to sit in God's presence, appreciating His nature and listening to what He wants to express. Keep a notepad beside you and note down anything that comes to mind—whether it be His ideas or yours. Keeping the line of communication free of brain clutter and distractions, let this time be a gift to God, set apart to commune with Him, being filled by Him.

NATURALISTIC

Consider the most beautiful scenery you've encountered in your life. If you can, visit this place in person or recollect it in your mind. Ask Jesus to reveal where He is in this place and how He is with you. In this time together, appreciate the moment and listen for what He is saying. Tell Him how you feel being in this place and what you appreciate about it.

> Then He said, "Hear now My words: If there is a prophet among you, I, the Lord, make Myself known to him in a vision; I speak to him in a dream.
>
> **NUMBERS 12:6 NKJV**

> After these things the word of the Lord came to Abram in a vision, saying, "Do not fear Abram, I am a shield to you, your reward shall be very great."
>
> **GENESIS 15:1 NASB1995**

On the next day, as they were on their way and approaching the city, Peter went up on the housetop about the sixth hour to pray. But he became hungry and was desiring to eat; but while they were making preparations, he fell into a trance; and he saw the sky opened up, and an object like a great sheet coming down, lowered by four corners to the ground.

ACTS 10:9-11 NASB1995

CHAPTER TWELVE

— Bless You —

*Bless you, one who has access to God's good
gifts through relationship with Him.*

Be blessed with knowing who you are in Him.

*Bless you with good gifts from God and the awareness
to appreciate them as they are given.*

*God bless you with the expressions of His great love
for you in ways that He knows you will love.*

God bless you with peace in your journey.

Be blessed with a relational intimacy between you and Father God.

*Bless you with increased trust in God's ability to bring
you want you need at the right time, and when.*

Be blessed with hearing from God in ways you understand.

*I bless you with the sweetness of knowing in your core that God is always
speaking to you and that He loves you so much more than you know.*

In Jesus' name,

Amen.

xxxxx

Chapter Thirteen

DREAMS

> "And afterward,
> I will pour out my Spirit on all people.
> Your sons and daughters will prophesy,
> your old men will dream dreams,
> your young men will see visions.
>
> **JOEL 2:28 NIV**

— Father's Heart —

As your body and mind rest at night, it is an ideal time for Me to speak life into your tired body.

Give Me all the cares of your day, My child. Then snuggle up and rest in Me.

As you become aware of My presence, welcome Me into your dreams and night time.

The day seems long at times, and your nights have been a struggle too. It's time to reclaim the night—if you will allow Me.

Trust Me to protect you as you sleep.

One way I speak to you is through dreams. I have always done this. I love to show you My heartbeat and reveal more about Myself during this special time together.

I will invest into you physically, so that you can walk in peace when you wake.

I enjoy showing you scenes of life as you dream. Some dreams will be practical, obvious things. Others will be symbolic, requiring you to ask Me for more clarity when you awaken. Others will be prophetic encouragements for the present and future.

In fact, sometimes you might feel like you have lived something before, as it is happening. This is because I gave you a dream about it.

I can give you answers to questions that have been troubling you. Dreams are a gift from My heart to yours.

As your body begins to wind down, and your mind follows, thank Me for being with you, and hand over your night time to Me.

During these times I love to pour refreshment into you, speak to you of things to come, and give you ideas to act upon.

I love to give you answers when you are finally still.

Trust me with your dream life and begin to take notice of what you go to sleep with and wake up with. Take note of the very first things you remember as you drop into sleep, and the very last things you remember just before you awaken.

These ideas can be powerful truths that bless both you and others.

Listen to My instruction and ask if you don't understand. As you seek Me, I will reveal all at the right time.

I am excited to think that you might invite My Holy Spirit to meet with you as you sleep. Share your night times with Me, beloved. Your sleep allows hours of uninterrupted listening time; I love it when I have your full attention, engaging with your heart.

As you hand over these times, trust Me to bring you goodness every step of the way.

I love you and I want the absolute best for you, My beloved.

DREAMS

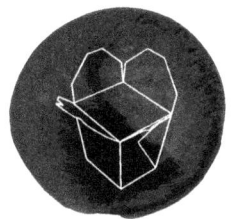

— Take Aways —

My sleep routine can impact my dreams and night time health.

The key thing with dreaming is to remember that God is for me. He is goodness to the core and whatever He brings to me is for my good, as well as for the benefit of others.

REFRAMING MY NIGHTS WITH GOD OPENS A WORLD OF POSSIBILITIES.

Entrusting my night-time to God is a great place to begin sleep.

Asking God to communicate with me throughout the night is powerful.

> God used dreams to uplift me when my body is weak, and I had nothing to offer anyone.

> Keeping a notebook beside the bed is helpful for sleepily recording anything significant He reveals.

> Night times and dreaming are about Spirit-to-spirit time—with Him.

> As I sleep/dream, it is an opportunity for God to finally have my full attention, with no interruptions, obstacles, or distractions.

> God can totally redeem any anxiety, fear, and dread at night-times through dreaming and rest with Him.

> To list the benefits of dreams is like trying to condense God into a single sentence—impossible.

DREAMS

> WHILE I SLEEP, THE SPIRITUAL ATMOSPHERE IS AWAKE AND THRIVING.

Dreams are just another way for God to communicate with me, giving His perspective through images, scenes, encounters or tending to my body, soul, and spirit.

I often pray for my family and friends who don't know God that He would meet them in their dreams.

When they come under the Lordship of Christ, dreams can be a life-giving key from God.

I have learnt that even when having a "bad dream," God has a redemptive message or insight at the heart of it.

Dreaming with God has a profound impact on my relationship with Him.

When sleep evades me, envision Jesus and ask to have an adventure with Him—then watching for what comes to mind. I quickly find myself in zzzz land, and when I don't, at least we've had some fun together in the meantime.

— Questions To Ponder —

1. Was there anything that leapt out about dreams and night times with God?

2. What do I believe about dreams and night time?

3. How would I describe my sleep habits? Do I remember my dreams? What experiences have I had with dreams? Have they been positive or negative experiences?

4. What has been my history of dreaming? What was my childhood like? What did my parents or caregivers tell me when I struggled to sleep or had nightmares? Ask God if there is anything He wants me to recall.

> To these four young men God gave knowledge and understanding of all kinds of literature and learning. And Daniel could understand visions and dreams of all kinds.
>
> **DANIEL 1:17 NIV**

CHAPTER THIRTEEN

5. Do I want God to use my night time for dreaming with Him? Why? Why not?

6. What biblical examples reveal that God speaks through dreams?

> "And it shall come to pass afterward, that I will pour out my Spirit on all flesh; your sons and your daughters shall prophesy, your old men shall dream dreams, and your young men shall see visions."
>
> **JOEL 2:28 ESV**

7. If I don't dream or sleep well, am I willing to make some significant, practical changes to help? These changes could include investing in creating healthy sleep-time routines, etc. (refer to Appendix 6.) Why or why not? Are there any stumbling blocks to this?

8. What do I need most in this season? Am I open to God speaking to me about this through dreams?

> If you lie down, you will not be afraid; when you lie down, your sleep will be sweet.
>
> **PROVERBS 3:24 ESV**

9. Is there anything holding me back from allowing God to use my night times for His purposes? What is at the heart of this? Ask God for greater clarification.

10. What benefits might come from being more open, intentional, and invitational with God about my night times? If God speaks to and invests in me through dreams, how might this help my current situation?

DREAMS

—Playlist—

How Majestic – Kari Jobe

We Say Yes – Housefires

As Sure as the Sun – Ellie Holcomb

Glorious Unfolding – Steven Curtis Chapman

Good Good Father – Chris Tomlin

Move Your Heart – Maverick City

I Can Only Imagine – Mercy Me

— Activations —

MUSICAL

Go on a night time sleep hygiene adventure. (refer to Appendix 6) Create a playlist or your own piece of music that will aid sleep. Ask Holy Spirit to guide your creation and exploration.

VISUAL

Paint, draw, sketch, sculpt a dream. Think about how dreams come to us. How does God bring us these gifts of the night? Create this in some visual form.

LOGICAL

Consider and explore the various purposes of dreams. Consider these elements: instructional, symbolic, encouraging, processing life events and things on the mind, revelatory, to help others, intercessory, healing, defragging the brain, refining. Are there any others you have discovered in your research? What have you experienced yourself?

BODILY/KINESTHETIC

Spend some time reflecting upon your sleep hygiene and night time habits. Ask God about these. Consider the suggestions/ideas in Appendix 6. Are there any tweaks God is encouraging you to engage with?

DREAMS

INTRAPERSONAL

Reflect upon how dreams have played a part in your life. If they haven't, consider the information in Appendix 6. Spend some time asking yourself and God more about dreaming at night. What is God saying?

LINGUISTIC/VERBAL

Write poem about the purpose of dreams or step inside a dream space and write what it feels like to be in a dream. Consider what you want your reader to feel as they read your writing. Will it be humorous? Thought-provoking? Heartfelt? Sad? Questioning? Reflective? Experiential? Or something that expresses a dream you have actually had?

INTERPERSONAL

Imagine meeting someone who has never dreamt. They want to dream but feel they can't or won't. How would you encourage this person? What might you pray? Ask Holy Spirit to reveal insight. How will you help them come to peace about their internal conflict?

NATURALISTIC

Lie under a cloud-filled sky and watch the clouds roll by or find somewhere warm and cosy in nature. Try the activation with breathing (mentioned in Appendix 6). Practice the skill of breathing with God.

Now when they had departed, behold, an angel of the Lord appeared to Joseph in a dream and said, "Rise, take the child and his mother, and flee to Egypt, and remain there until I tell you, for Herod is about to search for the child, to destroy him."

MATTHEW 2:13 ESV

DREAMS

— Bless You —

Bless you, one who has good sleep and dreaming in their future.

Be blessed with deeper revelation from God about your unique design and His plan for your sleep times.

God bless you with freedom and healing from those things that have tried to steal your dreams and peace at night.

Bless the atmosphere of your home with His presence.

God bless you with protection and angelic help as you sleep.

Bless you with answered prayer and greater connection with God through your night times.

Be blessed with knowing Psalm 91 as your night time promise.

God bless you with sweet, deep, sleep.

In Jesus' name,

Amen.

xxxxx

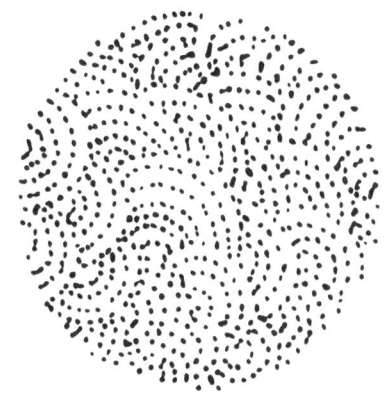

Chapter Fourteen

THANKFULNESS

Enter his gates with thanksgiving and his courts with praise; give thanks to him and praise his name.

PSALM 100:4 NIV

— Father's Heart —

My precious child, you are hardwired for thankfulness.

You have struggled under the heaviness of circumstances. At times it's been hard to see what you could be thankful for.

My heart longs for you to walk in thankfulness.

As you choose to say yes, stepping forward in intentional gratitude with Me, you trek a true faith walk.

When you walk with Me in thankfulness, you become more aware of Me in all things. You see Me in nature. You hear Me in relationship.

You experience Me as you were meant to—abundant life with Me.

Choosing to give thanks and recognising Me in situations is a step of trust and releases faith.

Faith brings change to everything; faith makes all things better.

It is so easy to see what you lack, yet I have given you much…and have so much more to bring.

It is waiting in the treasure trove of abundance, anticipating your choosing to trust Me for it. I love you that much.

I have My absolute best for you, My precious daughter. Don't doubt it for a second. It is coming and has indeed come.

This is the day I have made; rejoice and be glad in it!

By learning to live in a state of thankfulness, you experience My blessings more fully because you are more aware of My heart.

You crush the Enemy's plans by living in this way.

Start small and develop this skill. It takes practice and intentionality, but soon you'll find you can't help but see Me in it ALL.

You might feel like it isn't doing anything at the beginning but persist.

You will see how things around you change by giving thanks. It will change how you see the very things that have held you down for so long.

Each one is an opportunity to grow, yes, but also to flourish.

How much greater is faith when you can walk through fire and not be burned, because of your trust in Me!

Will you complain about the heat or thank Me for what I am bringing you through—all that I am overcoming in and through you.

The things of old will pale in comparison to that which I have for you, My child.

Walk through the fire, knowing all the while this will pass at some point. Ask Me how I see it, then watch, listen, and walk forward in the provision I have given you for this moment.

You WILL look back upon this time and see the benefits I have given you in it.

It is a time of blessing.

It is always a time to be thankful.

Thankfulness releases. It places hardship in its rightful place. It places Me in My rightful place—overcoming all.

Remember, I (the One Who overcomes all) am on your side.

THANKFULNESS

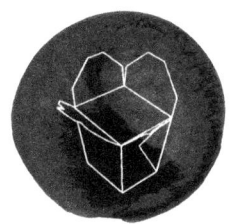

— Take Aways —

When I walk in the awareness of what I am experiencing, I can feel worse. When I walk in thanks (which reveals joy), I feel better. The circumstance may still exist, but my focus has shifted.

Thankfulness shifts the focus from me to Him.

IT ALLOWS ME TO TAKE THE FOCUS FROM MY SITUATION TO SOMETHING HIGHER.

Thankfulness can help build vulnerability in relationship, and safety.

There is always something for which I can be thankful.

CHAPTER FOURTEEN

> Thankfulness is a kingdom currency, rather than an earthly one.

> Thankfulness is a form of worship.

> Thankfulness is a powerful key to breakthrough.

> There is nothing to lose in fostering thankfulness (except maybe difficulty and loss).

I CAN EXPERIENCE OPPORTUNITIES FROM BEING THANKFUL..

> Gratefulness improves health—physical, psychological, mental, spiritual and emotional.

THANKFULNESS

WHAT AM I FOCUSED UPON?

Thankfulness releases good chemicals into my system.

Thankfulness releases the essence of God into situations and people.

Thankfulness develops an increased awareness of where my Heavenly Father has blessed me.

When I walk in thankfulness, things seem lighter and full of hope.

Fostering thankfulness helps to release appreciation into the everyday, which can help improve my relationships.

Thankfulness grows and generates hope.

A thankful heart crushes negativity.

CHAPTER FOURTEEN

— *Questions to Ponder* —

1. What is it that leaps out to me about the area of thankfulness?

2. What do I know about thankfulness and gratitude? What benefits do they bring to life? What is the opposite of being a person of gratitude? How might this impact my health and life?

THANKFULNESS

3. How do I know if I am a thankful person? What marks a person who is? What influences whether someone is thankful?

4. What fruit is gleaned from a life filled with gratitude?

Oh give thanks to the Lord, call upon His name; make known His deeds among the peoples.

1 CHRONICLES 16:8 ESV

5. Whilst still being authentic, how do I navigate hard seasons, people, and situations with a thankful heart? Are there any helps that I've observed? How do I do this well?

6. What does God say about thankful hearts in the word? How can this be applied to everyday life?

> O give thanks to the Lord, for He is GOOD; for His lovingkindness is everlasting.
>
> **1 CHRONICLES 16:34**
> **NASB 1995**

7. How does thankfulness play a part in my life today? Do I consider myself a thankful person? Have I always been this way? Is this an area in which I desire to grow?

8. What would those who love me best say about me? What parts of my design, personality, gifts, and skills, would they be thankful for?

I will bless the Lord at all times; His praise shall continually be in my mouth.

PSALM 34:1 NASB 1995

9. What are my favourite moments of thankfulness where I've experienced it from someone else and expressed it to others?

10. Are there any roadblocks to my fostering a thankful heart in this season? Ask God more about this.

> Be thankful in all circumstances, for this is God's will for you who belong to Christ Jesus.
>
> **1 THESSALONIANS 5:18 NLT**

THANKFULNESS

11. How would life look if I were to foster a heart of thankfulness in all things? How might it impact me? Those around me? Those who look up to me? Those who I come across in life?

Enter his gates with thanksgiving, and his courts with praise! Give thanks to him; bless his name!

PSALM 100:4 ESV

THANKFULNESS

Playlist

King of My Heart – John Mark and Sarah McMillan

Find Me – Jonathan David and Melissa Helser

Count Your Blessings – Johnson Oatman Jr. (1897)

Thank You Jesus – Hillsong Worship

Gratitude – Brandon Lake

I Thank God – Maverick City Music x Upper Room

You Have Made Me Glad – Charity Gayle

For the Good – Riley Clemmons

— *Activations* —

MUSICAL

Using a regular beat rhythm, declare the people, places, and things you are thankful for. Have a thankfulness session—a thankfest in song form.

VISUAL

Take some time to visit, connect with, or interact with your favourite places, people and things—photograph each one as you become aware of appreciating them, using these images to create a photographic blessing board. Each one represents something for which you are thankful. Let it be a reminder that you have much for which to be thankful in life.

LOGICAL

Explore the benefits of thankfulness. Check out the thankfulness project and other gratitude-based programs. Are there any aspects of what you have read about that you'd like to adopt? Why or why not?

BODILY/KINESTHETIC

Body thanks. How can you bless your body today? Consider all the working parts, the systems and functions that your body does to allow movement, connection and flourishing in life. Make a special date with your body to bless it in some form today—massage, rest, sleep, spa, swim, exercise, declaration, breathing, hydrating. Whatever you do, be intentional about blessing your body both in action and word.

INTRAPERSONAL

Create a thankfulness life timeline. Do this either by year, by decade, or by season. For each section, note down the highlights and thankfulness markers that come to mind. Ask Holy Spirit for reminders. Have some fun revisiting these special times of wonder and delight with God. Note what happens internally as you focus upon these.

LINGUISTIC/VERBAL

Ask God to highlight what and who you are thankful for. Write a personal handwritten letter to special people in your life. Consider how you feel about them and their special qualities that make the world a better place. Write about the impact their life has had upon yours, how you are better for having them in your life. Put this letter in an envelope and if you can, put it in the post and send it to them. Thoughtful acts like this mean the world to people with a words-of-affirmation love language.

INTERPERSONAL

Have a gratitude meal with some loved ones. Consider the people seated at the table and why you are thankful for them. Scatter pieces of paper around the table during the meal to encourage everyone to write down what they are grateful for over the past year. Guests will place the slips of paper in a large bowl in the middle of the table. Try to fill the bowl as the goal! When finished, spend some time reading these and thanking God around the table for these times.

NATURALISTIC

Think about one of your favourite places to to visit, people or animals that you are thankful for. How can you express thankfulness to them today? Consider encouraging, thanking, or blessing this special person, place or thing, through the gift of time, talent or treasure.

THANKFULNESS

— Bless You —

Bless you, one who has much to be thankful for in life.

God bless you with a thankful heart and mind.

Be blessed with wisdom to step into thankfulness.

*Bless your senses with the ability to engage
with God and gratitude at every turn.*

Be blessed with an ease in your thankfulness.

*God bless you with relational harmony and
an attitude of gratitude in them.*

Bless you with vision that can see the good in all circumstances.

Be blessed as you experience other's thankfulness of you in life.

*Bless you with increased encounters with the
fruit of intentional gratitude.*

In Jesus' name,

Amen.

xxxxx

Chapter Fifteen

LAMENT

Out of the depths I cry to you, O Lord!
O Lord, hear my voice! Let your ears be
attentive to the voice of my pleas for mercy!

PSALM 130:1-2 ESV

— Father's Heart —

Pour out your heart to Me, My precious one.

Leave nothing behind.

*I know the griefs of your heart and desire to help
you process all that has come against it.*

*Lament, bring your woes, your cares, your worries, and
pains—nothing is off-limits to bring to Me.*

I see the depths of grief, disappointments, and hurts, and I understand.

*I care more than you will ever know; let Me tend to you, beloved.
Let Me hold you close as you share from your innermost pain.*

*Leave nothing out. As you pour it out from heart and head
to Me, I will comfort and nurture you, My child.*

*I know you've tried to heal some hurts through external measures,
including counselling, ministry, forgiveness, and these have been good.
But residue—consequences of actions and pain—remains. Only I can
touch these depths, and I have My best available to you, beloved.*

*At times you have wondered whether you would ever see the end of this
roller coaster…take heart. There is hope as you share it with Me.*

*There is no rush to resolve or finish up the process, but for your
health, remember that sharing it with Me will help you.*

You have held it all together for so long. You've tried to do the "right" thing. At times, you've found it unbearable, wondering whether you would ever make it through. Please know that bringing your authentic self to Me (the person I already know and love) brings freedom to your heart and healing to your situation.

Some things will never resolve here on earth, BUT take heart, I have overcome the world.

When you reach the end of yourself, there I am.

I am with you always.

I know all, see all, and care.

You are not alone, My cherished one. Your pain is not your own; I am with you in it.

Come, let's put aside some time to meet and to share.

I am ready, willing, and able to listen.

Pour out your raw; leave nothing behind, My darling.

Then when you've emptied yourself of all that you've wanted to say, let Me tend to you.

Let Me apply balm to the wounds of life so that you might heal and have My peace in full once again.

LAMENT

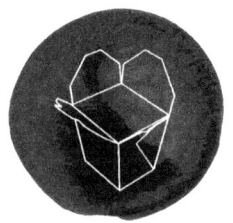

— Take Aways —

If I can't move past something and I feel stuck or powerless, lamenting can help.

In lament I don't need to consider others; it's simply about my experience of something.

I share it with God because even as I bring Him my pain, instead of judging me, He nods, embraces my heart, holds me, often saying little but expressing so much to those deep places.

Some circumstances require greater depths of healing than what I humanly know to do, but God does know!

Lament is a healing release.

CHAPTER FIFTEEN

Lament can be a way to express the depths of my pain inside in an external way.

Lamenting is a prophetic act of faith.

GOD HAS WAYS FOR MY SORROW TO BE RELEASED.

Lament is grieving, deep sorrow, and the expression of this anguish with God.

Lament invites God into my sorrow rather than keeping Him outside of it.

Lamenting validates my emotions, feelings, and experiences.

The Bible is filled with examples of this biblical strategy called lament.

LAMENT

Deciding to connect with God in my pain also invites Him to act on my behalf, touching my heart and situation.

LAMENTING WITH GOD LEADS ME BACK TO HOPE.

Lamenting is often an outward expression of an internal pain, sorrow or grief.

Lamenting is the intimate place where I am heard by Him, and He tends to my heart.

Expressions of lament are different for different people.

Lamenting helps me to come to God with my complaints, deep upsets, and sadness. I can share in safety with Him.

CHAPTER FIFTEEN

— Questions to Ponder —

Did something jump out to me about this area of lament?

What do I know/believe about lament?

LAMENT

1. What is the difference between lamenting and grieving?

2. What examples of lamenting do I find in the Scriptures? Are there specifics books which are filled with lament?

> "O our God, will you not execute judgment on them? For we are powerless against this great horde that is coming against us. We do not know what to do, but our eyes are on you."
>
> **2 CHRONICLES 20:12 ESV**

3. What do I notice about people who lamented in Scripture? Were there benefits for them? If so, is it possible that I could glean similar benefits? Why or why not?

4. Is there anything holding me back from lamenting? Are there any reasons I wouldn't lament? Why or why not?

LAMENT

5. Is there something in the present which feels too BIG for me to process by myself? Do I feel limited and frozen in time about any experience, sorrow, or hurt? Ask Father for some insight into this situation.

6. How in touch am I with my emotions, feelings, and inner world? Am I willing to allow God to reveal fresh levels of my inner world through lament?

> God, listen! Listen to my prayer, listen to the pain in my cries. Don't turn your back on me just when I need you so desperately. Pay attention! This is a cry for help! And hurry—this can't wait!
>
> **PSALM 102:1-2 MSG**

7. If lamenting removes walls between God and me, building greater intimacy between us, what does this mean for my circumstance or deep pain? How does this idea feel for my heart?

8. What advantages might lamenting about hard seasons bring to my life?

> Because of the Lord's great love we are not consumed, for his compassions never fail. They are new every morning; great is your faithfulness. I say to myself, "The Lord is my portion; therefore I will wait for him."
>
> **LAMENTATIONS 3:22-24 NIV**

LAMENT

—Playlist—

Wounds – Jordan Feliz

New Wine – Hillsong Worship

Prayer for the Earth – Mike Oldfield

Beautiful Jesus – Melissa Helser

Once and for All – Lauren Daigle

With You Now – Ellie Holcomb

New Wine – Hillsong Worship

Broken Vessels – Hillsong Worship

Starts and Ends – Hillsong Worship

Weep with Me – Rend Collective

Every Giant Will Fall – Rend Collective

Get Back Up – Toby Mac

Blessed Assurance – Fanny Crosby, New York City, USA (1873)

Bless the Broken Road – Rascal Flatts

— *Activations* —

--- MUSICAL ---

Put your sorrow and hurt to music. Express to God musically all that He prompts. Let the notes express each emotion, each situation, each point of pain. Forget the musical rules, and simply freestyle with God.

Listen to God's response to your expression.

Let your heart tinker in response to His heart.

Play and sing until an exchange has happened or until peace has landed.

--- VISUAL ---

Ask God to highlight an area He wants you to lament about.

Select an easily expressive art medium. Pour out your pain using your choice of art expression. Let it represent the intricacies of your sorrow. Leave nothing out. If you wish, do the same with God's response to your artwork.

Ignore the so-called art rules, what you know to be "right," and simply create with Him.

Let this piece reflect your depths and disappointments, and if led—God's response to your pain.

LAMENT

LOGICAL

Research biblical lamenting, observing how people lamented and what followed their cries, as well as God's responses. Explore how lamenting is done in current day. What is common to these examples of lamenting? Has anything changed? If you needed to explain lament to someone who knew nothing, what would you say? How could what you have discovered impact you?

BODILY/KINESTHETIC

Let your body represent any inner conflicts, hurts, and pains.

Express these before the Lord. Physically cry out as you feel led.

Keep pouring out with your body until you sense you've nothing left to say/express.

Now lie down. Let your body rest as you take time to hear all that God wants to say in response.

INTRAPERSONAL

Spend some time with God, asking Him to highlight something He wants you to lament with Him about. Ask Him for a time frame.

Ask Him to reveal how He wants you to lament.

LINGUISTIC/VERBAL

Write your own psalm based upon this season of life.

Attune your heart to God's presence as you write. Pour out all innermost feelings, beliefs, and words. Hold nothing back from God.

Once you've poured out all, take some time to listen and write down God's response to your sorrow.

INTERPERSONAL

Talk with a friend who is familiar with this idea of lamenting and how lamenting might help you in this season. Develop a plan of next steps with your trusted friend. Pray together.

NATURALISTIC

Consider how nature grieves. How does flora and fauna respond to loss, sorrow, or grief? What examples can you see or find? How can this observation help you in your own sorrow?

"I will repay you for the years the locusts have eaten—
the great locust and the young locust,
the other locusts and the locust swarm—
my great army that I sent among you.
You will have plenty to eat, until you are full,
and you will praise the name of the Lord your God,
who has worked wonders for you;
never again will my people be shamed.
Then you will know that I am in Israel,
that I am the Lord your God,
and that there is no other;
never again will my people be shamed."

JOEL 2:25-27 NIV

CHAPTER FIFTEEN

— Bless You —

Bless you, one who is never alone in whatever you walk.

God bless your heart during times of loss and times of laughter.

*Bless your heart with the freedom to share with the One
Who has walked alongside you every step of the way.*

*Be blessed with knowing that God has not left
you, but is present here in this place with you.*

*Bless you, precious one, with clarity of heart and mind as you share
your all with God. Bless you with not holding anything back.*

God bless you with experiencing His safety as you pour out your pain.

*Bless you with clarity, healing, and shalom
as He responds in love to your trust.*

*God bless you with knowing He is collecting every
tear and cares more than you ever realised.*

Bless you with freedom and release as you process your griefs with Him.

In Jesus' name,

Amen.

xxxxx

Chapter Sixteen

LIVING LEGACY

I have fought the good fight, I have finished the course, I have kept the faith.

2 TIMOTHY 4:7 NASB1995

— Father's Heart —

My beloved one, a legacy is not just for after you've come home, when the earthly body is dust.

I give you the gift of a living legacy, and it is for now.

A life that takes My hand, inviting you to journey with Me, leaving a life legacy everywhere we go.

This living legacy invests in others' lives—present and future—and allows you to see the impact of your life as we travel together.

You might not see it straight away, but you'll see how the threads entwine, and ultimately create something beautiful, something you can be proud of, something that lifts, loves, and shares beyond what you might have ever chosen for yourself.

Sometimes it might require a letting go of good to step into My best. Take heart; I have a legacy for you that is beyond what you have planned for yourself.

I consider all that you have been through and will go through, and make it shine with redemptive threads of life. I did this before the beginning of time.

Past, present, or future, time is not My concern. I know as challenges and circumstances beyond your control arise, you worry about the future.

My beloved, you know that I have promised you a future of hope, purpose, and joy!

CHAPTER SIXTEEN

Trust Me! Let go of those things you hold tighter than Me.

Are you willing to release all that holds your heart and instead take My hand in trust?

Step by step, little by little, you'll soon discover that the very things that came along were actually positioning you for life abundant. Any hard thing you walk through WILL accomplish something good because My heart is as ultimate redeemer.

There is purpose in all things. No, I don't send it all to you, but I WILL use it both for your good and for the good of others. I love to turn things around miraculously.

My story of your life is so much better. Yes, you can settle for good, or leap into My best for you. Which will you choose?

I know you. I understand your heart. I love how I created you to be; now let Me guide you into unexplored territories.

Let's adventure together afresh. Let Me unveil the main event in your life, and watch—watch what I do with a heart that is willing to let it all go to come in step with Me.

I can't help but smile as I think upon all I have planned for us in our together story.

I will never force it upon you, beloved. I offer it to you today—no strings attached. You can choose to reject My offering; but don't worry, I'll still love you 100 percent.

Or you can choose to embrace what I offer you—My hand, My heart, and a life so filled with Me that you'll wonder if heaven has indeed come to earth.

Whatever you choose, know that I am for you! I love you! I will never, ever, ever, ever leave you.

Let's adventure together into fresh beginnings, My child, leaving a living legacy along the path for others to find.

LEGACY

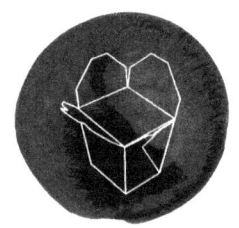

— Take Aways —

It feels so much better to release the things that have plagued our hopes and dreams and place them in the best hands possible.

What if I asked different questions? Instead of asking "Why me?" ask "What are You doing in this, Lord?"

MY LIFE STORY MATTERS.

God has taken my past trauma, pain, and story and uses it for good.

He wants to turn my past into victorious legacies of good.

He is worthy of handling the heavy things that have drained me.

The things that cause me to struggle are often the very things that bring the greatest fruit and act as a springboard for me and those who follow.

Prioritising God is always the best decision. Taking His hand in whatever.

GOD IS THE KING OF REDEMPTION. HE WANTS TO TURN THE DIREST OF EXPERIENCES INTO GOOD FOR ME.

My story can leave a legacy of life with those to come. What will be my legacy? What gift do I want to give the world? What does God say my purposes are?

The very things designed to pull me away from God and from faith can indeed draw me closer to Him and have a positive rippling impact.

LEGACY

He has so much good in store for me and His realised promise is only moments away. God always brings the promise of new hope in every circumstance.

I GET TO LEAVE MY WORRIES WITH HIM AND JOIN IN THE BEST STORY THE WORLD HAS EVER KNOWN: HIS STORY OF MY LIFE.

What if this hard thing is realigning me to God's best? Would it make it easier to bear if this was true?

Who and what I partner with, will be outwardly expressed in my life.

There is a choice to be made. I can allow the things of the past to determine my present and future. Or I can release those things that bind and burden to the One Who knows the way through.

— Questions to Ponder —

1. Was there anything that leapt out to me about living legacy?

2. When I think about leaving a legacy, what do I think this means? What does a living legacy mean to me?

> To obtain an inheritance which is imperishable and undefiled and will not fade away, reserved in heaven for you.
>
> **1 PETER 1:4 NASB1995**

3. What kinds of examples of legacies have I seen? Has someone's legacy impacted my life? Who do I have in my life right now who is leaving a living legacy to me?

4. How do I view my story? If I were to write it all down, what would be the high and low points? Are there themes in my life story? Things that have happened repeatedly? What are the God themes in my life story?

> And now I commend you to the care of God and to the message of his grace, which is able to build you up and give you the blessings God has for all his people.
>
> **ACTS 20:32 GNT**

5. What does God say about me, to me? Is there any part of my life He wants me to let go of or change? (Ask Him if I haven't asked recently.)

6. Who writes my life story? Am I pleased with what it looks like? Would I like to change anything for the future?

> For I know the plans I have for you, declares the LORD, plans for welfare and not for evil, to give you a future and a hope.
>
> **JEREMIAH 29:11 ESV**

7. "The past is the past and that can't change, but the present and the future are wide open spaces to be written upon."– Karen Brough. Do I agree with this statement? Why or why not? How might I adapt it to reflect my beliefs?

8. Is there something I would like to impart to the world and those around me? What messages does my life story tell? Am I willing to embrace a living legacy from God?

> A good person leaves an inheritance for their children's children, but a sinner's wealth is stored up for the righteous.
>
> **PROVERBS 13:22 NIV**

9. Are there any roadblocks to my saying yes to God's living legacy, or for my story to be redeemed? Ask God more about this possibility.

10. If I viewed my life through the eyes of the angels who cheer me on from the sidelines, would it feel differently? Hebrews 12:1 NLT

> I remember your genuine faith, for you share the faith that first filled your grandmother Lois and your mother, Eunice. And I know that same faith continues strong in you.
>
> **2 TIMOTHY 1:5 NLT**

LEGACY

11. What benefits would there be in this season of life if I began to live it with God's viewpoint of my story? What would remain and what would change if I chose to say yes to living legacy? What fruit might it bring?

We will not hide them from their children, but tell to the coming generation the glorious deeds of the Lord, and his might, and the wonders that he has done. He established a testimony in Jacob and appointed a law in Israel, which he commanded our fathers to teach to their children, that the next generation might know them, the children yet unborn, and arise and tell them to their children,

PSALM 78:4-6 ESV

LEGACY

— Playlist —

Tapestry – Hillsong United

Write Your Story – Francesca Battistelli

Build My Life – Housefires

Life Is a Gift – Hillsong Worship

My Story – Hillsong United

Wonder – Hillsong United

Goodbye Ordinary – Mercy Me

Talking to Jesus – Elevation Worship and Maverick City

Who You Say I Am – Hillsong

Open Space — Housefires

The Potter's Hand – Darlene Zschech

— Activations —

MUSICAL

Write or compose a piece of music or rhythm that tells a piece of your story—one of redemption and hope. Express the beginning, middle and end of the story. Ask Holy Spirit for His leading in creating it.

VISUAL

Visually express a moment in time where God redeemed something that seemed impossible to fix. It should lift, invest hope, and inspire. Ask God for His view of it.

LOGICAL

Make a list of people from Biblical times who walked a life as living legacies. What were the markers of their lives? What is consistent in them? How did God interact with them? How did He redeem their stories?

BODILY/KINESTHETIC

Jeremiah 29:11 ESV, "For I know the plans I have for you… to give you a future and a hope" Express this life verse using your body and movement in dance or body sculpture.

LEGACY

INTRAPERSONAL

How do I respond when things don't go as planned? Explore the intricacies of your responses in the past, and ask God for some fresh strategies to help in the future. Ask Him if there is anything He wants you to release to make way for His best.

LINGUISTIC/VERBAL

Write a legacy of declaration for the future. As you collect the ideas for this piece, consider where you've come from, what you've experienced, God's position in this—and how you want to walk in the future. Answer this question: what do I want my living legacy to be for those around me?

INTERPERSONAL

Spend some time with God. Journal, talk, or think about your life with Him. Share with Him those things that grieve your heart. Ask Him what He wants to talk about today. Then ask Him about His version of that same event. Ask Him more questions about it. Let it be a conversation of the heart. Ask Him how He wants to redeem it?

NATURALISTIC

Consider planting a garden or plot of space with something that will help feed and tend to others. Leave a legacy of life and love to those who might enjoy the benefits of this space. If you don't have it available, consider tidying up a neighbour's garden as a gift, or volunteer at your local community hub or church. As you tend the garden, envision the space's being a metaphor for what God does with the hard seasons of your life.

CHAPTER SIXTEEN

— Bless You —

Bless you, one who has a legacy that impacts others for good!

God bless you with the ability to see your story through His eyes.

Bless you with wisdom and discernment to bring every season to Him.

Be blessed with courage to stand firm against whatever is thrown at you because He is with you and has good plans for you.

Bless your trust levels with His increase, and your life with His flourish.

God bless your story with His redemptive touch.

Bless you with a heart of celebration and anticipation as you look at what God is doing within the messy parts of life.

Be blessed with growing hope in your story.

Bless those who come along your path with conversations, connections, and interactions that lift the both of you and leave you wanting more of God.

In Jesus' name,

Amen.

xxxxx

BONUS CHAPTER

Adoration of God

This book series has been a wild, life-altering, challenging, heart-wrenching, wonderful, personal, intricate, overwhelming, miraculous journey at EVERY turn.

There is nothing special about me, but Him in me….and although hard in so many ways, I know that many have been touched as He's allowed them to feel seen, heard, and validated in hard seasons.

This was the book I needed and still need as I heal and draw near to Him Who created me.

I felt it was fitting to pop in a bonus chapter of adoration, an agendaless thank you chapter for God.

Without Him, this book would not exist, nor would you or I.

Enjoy this final chapter of bits and pieces where we aim to bring a gift as we adore the One and Only; King of kings; Miracle Worker; Healer; Helper; Comforter; Prince of Peace; Master; Lord of lords; Holy One; Restorer; Saviour; Good Shepherd; Advocate; Protector; my Way, Truth, and Life; Light of the World; Blesser; Giver; Warrior; Companion; Answer; Strong Tower; Ultimate Redeemer; Counsellor; Shield; Rock; Lifegiver; Anchor; True Vine; Messiah; Bright Morning Star; Branch; Source; Replenisher; Servant; Heart of the Father; High Priest; Intercessor; Lamp; Creator; and Friend.

Jesus, Holy Spirit, and Father God, we adore You.

We love Who You are and all that You reflect to us.

Life simply isn't right without You.

We appreciate all that You have done for us, but more than that,

Thank You for all that You are…

ADORE
KAREN BROUGH © 2022

Your kindness, gentleness, humour, and love,
Your faithfulness, patience, and power from above.

Your goodness, mercy, perfection, and grace—
Your heart which longs for us to see Your face.

All knowing, unchanging and complete one in all,
Your heart only asking us to answer Your call.

You're wise, discerning, humble, worry free…
In my life story here, there's nothing You don't see.

Your solid foundation to breath You—like air,
All-powerful, all-loving and indeed everywhere.

In life's mysteries, challenges, You are a hope key,
In my turmoil and strife, Your eyes remain fixed on me.

As we share with You, we know we've been heard
As You work in good ways; all it takes is Your Word.

You're glorious, beautiful, creative, and great,
Unwilling to allow mankind to reap its fate.

Merciful, kind, and compassionate too,
Your vision—higher, better and a more complete view.

Forgiving, just, and so full of grace,
Arms outstretched wide for the whole human race.

Holy, set apart, no one like You, Oh Lord,
One part of three—three strands make a cord.

You're good, faithful, just, and true,
Your heart, Your nature beyond description—You!

Abounding in love, giving generously without fuss,
Timeless, sufficient, yet You reach out for us.

You see all, know all, care when we're low,
Nothing escapes Your notice—not even a sparrow.

"We love you" seems too small as You are so true,
You love us in full—to our fractured parts; You are glue.

BONUS CHAPTER

Adoration of Him

Remember – Maverick City Music

O Come Let Us Adore Him – Maverick City Music, featuring Chandler Moore and Jekalyn Carr

O Praise the Name – Kristene DiMarco

O Come, O Come Emmanuel – Maverick City Music, featuring Naomi Raine and Nate Moore

Echo Holy – Red Rocks Worship

Heart of the Father – Ryan Ellis

The Reason – Wilder/TRBL Music

APPENDIX 1

Below is a brief list of opposite spirit feelings or words that might help to get you started in what can be experienced with God as He makes exchanges with us.

RAW EMOTION	GOD'S REDEMPTIVE VERSION (OPPOSITE)
Hate	Love, affection, treasure, cherish
Unforgiveness	Forgiveness, grace, compassion, open arms of love
Fear	Trust, hope, faith, community, safety, comfort, courage, peace, exchanging our heaviness for His light
Anxiety/Worry	Trust, fearlessness, faith, release, support, reassurance, calm, hope, comfort, joy
Anger	Gentleness, peace, patience, self-control, calm, comfort, joy, delight
Hopelessness	Hope, trust, faith, delight, anticipation of good, expectancy of good, healing
Depression/Heaviness	Trust, faith, peace, release, lifting eyes up, contentment, joy, hopefulness, thankfulness
Rejection	Acceptance, love, warmth, comfort, approval, love, embrace, support, security, a place of welcome

RAW EMOTION	GOD'S REDEMPTIVE VERSION (OPPOSITE)
Isolation/Loneliness	Community life, He is always with us, joy, befriended, accepted, accompanied, embraced
Control	Submission to God and His ways, trust in Him, relinquish, freedom, let go, finding ourselves in a place of enough, liberated, unconstrained, contented
Despair/Discouragement	God's acceptance, God's truth, joy, peace, anticipation is built, encouragement, filled up, hope, supported, comforted, lifted
Guilt	Jesus having died on the cross with all our sin, forgiveness, freedom, innocent, blameless, virtuous, honoured, refreshed, light
Affliction/Poor health	Perfect health, fullness of the Holy Spirit within, freedom, trust, healthy, carefree, lighter hopeful, soothed, comforted, healed, tended to, supported, strong, provided for, whole
Pride	Submission to God and His leading, humility, release of control, modest, freedom, thankfulness, grace, innocent, peace, true security
Insecurity	Trust, security, strength, fearlessness, stable, assurance, courage, protection, safe, firm, assured, unafraid, released, free
Tempted	Strength, trust, truth, submission to God, released, courage, assured, secure, wisdom
Shame	Honoured, released, free, restored dignity, respected,

APPENDIX 2

Prayer Starters

PRAYER STARTERS WHICH HELP ME TO CLARIFY, ENCOURAGE, EXCHANGE OR CHANGE:

- God, renew my mind to be aligned with Yours.

- I choose to trust You, God, with _____.
  I release it to you now in Jesus' powerful name.

- Give me your heart, Father God, for _____. Help me to see them as You do.

- Precious Holy Spirit, please show me how You see me rather than what I feel or see now.

- Lord, I choose to roll off all heaviness now sitting on my shoulders and roll it onto Yours. Please take the heaviness, Lord, and replace it with Your _____ (opposite).

- Lord, please fill the gap between what they need and what I am right now.

- Father, please help me experience Your presence. I am not alone right now because You are here with me.

- Lord, give me a greater revelation of Your truth.

- Father, please give me a picture of what this situation looks like to You.
- Holy Spirit, please show me the lies I am believing about this situation.
- What is Your truth about this situation, Father?
- Jesus, please show me where you are in relation to me.
- Lord, I don't have the answer to this problem. Please show me Your answer.

APPENDIX 3

Blessing/Cursing

BLESSING	CURSING
Blessing is life giving.	Cursing and lack brings isolation.
Always affirms	It brings bitterness and conflict.
Increases energy levels	It allows others to feel threatened and alone.
Releases more blessing	It doesn't consider individual difference or strengths.
Recognises God's unique design of us: empowers and celebrates it	It always focuses on weakness.
Brings peace and contentment	It preys upon the weak and looks to devour them.
Lifts and encourages	It is often about control and manipulation.
Blessing someone releases them into God's care.	It is forced and negative.
Communal and relationship building	It speaks death and lack.
Celebrates strengths of others and releases them to be used mightily	It kills hope.
Is loving	It offers no future.
Changes behaviour, not through force, but through the leading of Holy Spirit	It only brings out the worst.
Is gentle and full of grace	It comes to kill, steal, and destroy. (This sounds like something I have heard before.
Is God's heart for life with one another	

APPENDIX 4

Joy

"Heaven is filled with absolute, perfect, confidence in God. This world is filled with absolute mistrust. And you and I will always reflect the nature of the world we are most aware of. What you live conscious of is what you will reproduce in the world around you. I try to live in such a way that nothing ever gets bigger in my awareness than my conscious awareness of the presence of God upon me."

BILL JOHNSON,
Manifesto for a Normal Christian Life

APPENDIX 5

The Word

When I asked Holy Spirit about the Word and the importance of getting into it, He gave me a picture of two scuba divers:

> They find themselves deep under the ocean with fish swimming about, caves, a shipwreck, and bubbles being released all around. One diver decides to take off his mask and his breathing apparatus. He believes he can swim more freely around without the burden of the heavy air tanks and gear. Without the weight of the uncomfortable tanks, he can easily explore the shipwreck and caves. Diving will be so much better without that gear!
>
> Initially he is right, he can swim more freely for a few seconds or even a minute or two. Then, reality begins to hit! His face is stricken, his eyes grow bigger, and panic starts to set in. He has a choice to allow the water to enter his lungs and drown or swim madly back to his gear and breathe the fresh air once again. He chooses the air this time. His body begins to calm as oxygen flows through his body once more. An experience like that is not easily forgotten.
>
> The other diver has been in scuba heaven: she has had access to life-giving air the entire time. Sharks came along and other dangers, but she was able to swim to safety with the proper gear and enough air in her tanks to sustain her.

The air in those tanks are pictures God's Word. Without it, we can survive for a short while. Then when life hits, we have a choice: allow it to overcome us or swim madly back to the tanks. God's Word is life giving! It is just one of the ways God communicates with us, and if we don't frequently breathe in His air, our oxygen will run out quickly. The air can become stale around us, and the things of this world will eventually overcome us.

Keep in the Word of God! Surround yourself entirely. When we swim in it, the richness of our lives increases dramatically. And the realisation that the cumbersome/heavy tanks, were light and well fitting for us all along. God's truth will be in the forefront of our minds, which means the lies of the Enemy are all the more obvious.

APPENDIX 6

Sometimes we are unable to recall our dreams because we shut down from them in childhood. This can happen through many ways:

1. Asking God to reveal if there is anything stopping you from remembering your dreams is a good place to start.

2. The parents of some have told them, "It's just a dream; it's not real" and other such statements, trying to bring comfort during a tumultuous time. The problem with this approach is that we inadvertently agree with those words and come to doubt dreams as being real. This can cause blockages to dreams with God.

3. If I had nightmares, I steadily learned how to block dreams, creating patterns and habits that don't engage with them, which includes wonderful God dreams.

   - Sample prayer: "God, I'm sorry for agreeing with these things which have blocked my dreaming with You. I forgive _____. I forgive myself as well for agreeing with these ideas. They were not true. Please reinstate my imagination and dream life. I want to hear You through my nighttime and dreams. In Jesus' name, amen."

   - This can help to open this area of communication with Him.

SLEEP HYGIENE/NIGHT TIME ROUTINE IDEAS

- Turn off technology and the television before you plan to go to bed. I find I need at least half an hour to an hour for turning off the television. For me, turning off the phone is much, much earlier because it emits a different light that ramps up the body.

- Listening to calming music, worship music, or classical music has been proven to help encourage sleep.

- Take a warm bath or shower.

- Journal or share with God all that is on your mind. I personally have a notebook where I defrag a little with Him before bed, especially when it's been a full day.

- Make peace with those you haven't.

- Action the things you can control. If that list is too long, write it down so it's out of your brain and ready to action tomorrow. Forgive others who He brings to mind and be forgiven by Him for those areas that are your growth areas.

- Ask Holy Spirit to cleanse the room/house.

- Ask Jesus to cover everything with His cleansing blood.

- Welcome God's peaceful presence.

- The following exercise may sound funny, but trust me, it can work, especially if the body is racing. Place your hands on either side of your navel and breathe, becoming aware of pushing your belly button up and then exhaling enough so your fingertips touch in the middle. This exercise helps the vagus nerve to be activated and invites in a more peaceful posture. Isn't God amazing how He has designed our bodies!

- Time to relax with Him and step into that peaceful place.

- If anything comes to mind, quickly note it in your notebook and get back into the rest place. Acknowledging these thoughts can often compound, increase, and hijack peace. If you find that thoughts keep coming and they are more distracting than helpful, ask God to guide your thoughts to a peaceful place of His choosing.

- Look/sense/feel what He is showing you.

- Become aware of your inner workings and how He has made your body.

- As you breathe, foster a thankfulness for these systems and anything else that comes to mind.

- Don't start heavy, big discussions with others heading into the sleep zone.

- Do say, "I love you" and bless one another.

- "God, you've got the next nine hours to connect with me in any way You like. Remove anything that might stop that from happening. Amen." For me, following these guidelines is how He began to speak through dreams.

EXPLANATION OF THE AUTUMN LEAF ON THE COVER

"I am the branches; you are the leaf.

Come, connect to My life-giving branches once again.

Let Me pour life back into you.

Let Me restore your color.

Let Me hold you once again.

*My arms are open wide and ready to
embrace your battle-weary form.*

*In the natural, a young leaf is green, full of hope and
life. The elements seem to come relentlessly.
Eventually, the wind, rain, and storms wear it down,
and the now colorless frail leaf falls from the tree lifeless.*

But with Me, this isn't the end, but the beginning.

I am counter-cultural and counter-intuitive.

*Where you may feel that your situation
has sucked the best years from you,*

That all is hopeless.

That there is no coming back from this place of upheaval,

Take heart with Me. This is not the case!

*You come to Me, dry, brittle, worn-out and weary,
and I pour Myself into those desert places.*

As I hold you, I pour My life into you.

I apply balm to your well-trodden, wilderness areas.

I restore your color.

I give you back life and bright eyes.

I lead you to green places of flourish.

*Where the world saps the life from you,
I give you life and life to the full.*

Take heart, My precious one, I am not limited by what you see or feel—there is HOPE and much future to be had.

You can come back from this and thrive with Me.

My beloved, this isn't the end of you, but the beginning of something new in you as you allow Me to embrace you once again."

"How does an autumn leaf relate to being held?

I think You just answered me, Father. Thank You."

ENCOURAGEMENT FOR THOSE ON A
Spiritual Journey
WHO WANT TO CONNECT WITH GOD FOR THEMSELVES

First, welcome; thank you for picking up my book.

You could have looked at countless books; I'm thankful that you landed here. Whatever led you here, I am confident that it's no mistake. This page is just for you if you are on a spiritual journey and want to know more about and encounter God for yourself.

No doubt, God has some encouragement for you—yes, even in your own challenging time. He loves all people, and the good news is that it includes us both. You've read some of my experiences with Him through this book, and no doubt you'll have your own to share as well.

If we met in everyday life, we'd probably be sitting down with a cuppa (cup of tea/coffee) and having a good conversation about life, faith, and whatever else came up.

We'd possibly share about our tough seasons and our challenges, but also the incredible things—those unexplainable moments which can only come from something outside of ourselves—that have happened along the way. These kinds of encounters are exciting to hear and to talk about with one another.

I'd be celebrating your unique God design and cheering you on in your journey. I love nothing better than doing this with whoever God brings along my path.

I know that you'd leave having been encouraged by Him, and I'd feel blessed for having met you. Although I appreciate your being here and taking a bold step forward in faith and exploration, this obviously isn't our meeting in person, which got me to thinking, *How does this happen through the pages of a book? How do I encourage someone I might never meet or talk with? What advice would I give to those who want to know God for themselves?*

So I began asking God for some advice. What steps do I take that have helped me connect with Him best? He answered me through a dream, and I wrote down the five steps He showed me.

1. BEGIN.

When I say *begin*, I mean start asking God to speak in a way that you understand.

Start talking to Him about everything. If you have questions, ask them.

Nothing is off-limits when it comes to talking to God.

Talking to God can be implemented through speaking verbally, journaling, or thinking with Him. Our "hows" do not limit Him, He is more interested in connecting rather than how you choose to connect with Him. He wants to be heard as much as you want to hear Him.

2. FOSTER AN AWARENESS OF HIM.

Keep watch, wait and take note of what He is saying, showing you, and how you sense He is communicating with you in the everyday.

Some of the ways He speaks are found in this book series, but there are sooooooo many more. Chances are, He has already been talking to you. You might not have recognized that God's voice doesn't necessarily sound like a Morgan Freeman voiceover, mystical, loud, or booming.

His voice can be the voice you hear in the quiet—the gentle prompting. Or when you feel your heart respond to something, this can be His Spirit leading you.

If you've ever felt or experienced love, joy, peace, kindness, patience, goodness, hope, or any other life-giving aspect, this IS God speaking. Without Him, these virtues would not exist.

Has something drawn your eye? Has something out of the ordinary happened? God is often in these too.

Nothing is off-limits when it comes to how God can communicate with you. Take note of those times when you are tended to, encouraged, or lifted. These kinds of help bear the heart of God.

Once you start noticing Him and taking note of His voice, you'll see He is always present and speaking with you.

3. START READING.

Get yourself a Bible or use a bible app. Plenty of options are available; I have found YouVersion is a great resource.

Start with the book of Mark. It talks about the life of Jesus, and none of this means anything without Jesus.

When exploring online, a plethora of options are available. How do we navigate this with wisdom? I find it's healthy to ask questions about anything I read:

- Is what I'm reading reflecting Jesus' heart and nature?
- Is it supported by the teachings of the Bible?
- Does it draw me closer to God and a healthy relationship with Him?

If it does all these things, then you are off to a good start.

4. FIND YOUR KIND OF PEOPLE.

We all need one another, so look out for and connect with a healthy local church or Christian community where we can grow together and encourage one another.

Ask God to show you where to start.

Understand that most churches differ in terms of worship styles and some beliefs. It's good to find one which fits how God has designed you to connect with Him.

5. CHECK OUT THE ALPHA WEBSITE.

This site (alpha.org.au) is a safe place to ask all those nagging questions and to wrestle with the significant issues. It's also an excellent resource for further information about Jesus and becoming a Christian.

God doesn't require you to work or strive to be loved by Him. He doesn't require you to be good enough to have a relationship with Him. He naturally wants to reveal Himself to those who want to get to know Him.

He's incredibly personal and wholly relational, and best of all, whether you know Him, He loves you 100 percent. Nothing you could do will ever change this unconditional love of His. It's great news!

I will be praying that your spiritual journey will be the best adventure of your life.

However you choose to take the next step, know that He is closer than you think, cares about you and all that you are going through, and has ways for you to flourish despite circumstances.

I hope you will thoroughly enjoy getting to know Father God in the way He has planned for you. I know it'll bless your life; I know this because I've lived the truth of it for decades. Woah, that makes me feel really old. Lol! But it's true!

God bless you, precious one; I'll be praying for you.

xxxxx

ABOUT THE AUTHOR

Karen Brough is an Australian wife, mother, writer, and former primary school teacher. She is the author of the *Be Held by Him* series, *Finding God when Life Knocks You Off Your Feet* and is currently working on some children's books with heart (and funny bone)—she is very excited to share updates with her subscribers—**karenbrough.com**

Ten years ago, when hit by a mystery illness, Karen began sharing the encouragements God gave her via her blog.

Her unique voice makes her readers feel understood, inspired, hopeful and encouraged. She spurs others on to connect with Father God for themselves by sharing the adventures she has with Him in everyday life.

Karen has always had a passion for writing and for encouraging others and cannot remember a time without this. Her blog has been read and enjoyed both domestically and internationally.

She loves nothing better than to spend time with her husband and three children. In warmer months, you'll often find her body boarding and making sand castles at the beach; or lying by the pool doing crosswords and creating "healthy" gelato for anyone who might drop by.

In cooler weather, she loves jigsaws, rom coms, bubble baths and baking anything warm, comforting and delicious—often hiding vegetables in sweet muffin recipes, much to her children's disgust. (Secretly they love it though.) She is still yet to find the perfect dairy free gelato recipe.

She loves the slower, unhurried pace of life and following this past health-challenge season, desires God's peace above all else.

She loves to laugh, cry and love with her whole heart, and wants to leave this earth a whole lot better than when she came into it. She loves nothing better than to help others see their value and worth, and help them fly to even greater heights in life, love and faith.

> Nevertheless, I will bring health and healing to it; I will heal my people and will let them enjoy abundant peace and security.
>
> **JEREMIAH 33:6 NIV**

CONNECT WITH US

We Love to hear from readers: If you have been impacted by this book, please consider getting in touch with us.

or

Leave a review on Amazon or Goodreads, so others can benefit from your personal experience. (this also helps get the word out about the books)

It takes a village to make the world go round, and you are an important part of our village.

FREE RESOURCES FOR MY READERS:
KARENBROUGH.COM/REGISTER

FACEBOOK: KARENBROUGHAUTHOR

INSTAGRAM: KARENBROUGHAUTHOR
KARENBROUGHKIDS

WEBSITE: KARENBROUGH.COM

Writing can be quite an isolating space, so we LOVE hearing from you.

Has the book impacted your life; your relationship with God?

Do you have a testimony of His goodness in your own hard time?

Or if you have any encouragements, fan art or inspirational creations that might help inspire or affirm others, share and connect with your online village on the "Be Held by Him" Facebook page or email us at **beheldbyhimseries@gmail.com**

GOD BLESS YOU DEARLY, BRAVE ONE.

FINAL WORD

Precious Reader,

It's with a touch of sadness that I see the end of this series, it has truly been a work of heart, tears, patience, and vulnerability. It has cost me greatly at times, but on the flip side, has also given me so much fruit as well.

I pray it has given you a gift along the way too.

I am looking forward to future writing projects (as prompted by Him), and in the meantime, there is still plenty to share, and to celebrate—and I do this on my website and social media. If you liked these kinds of stories, I blog these regularly at karenbrough.com.

I love hearing from my readers and always try to respond personally to each and every letter.

For those who have already reached out, thankyou for your kind words, your stories that have come about as a result of reading the series. Your testimonies of His fingerprint in your lives have been like honey for my heart—these encourage me greatly!

Let's never give up in being wowed by His goodness in it all.

God bless you and keep you, make His face shine upon you, and give you peace.

Much love,
Karen
xxxxx

P.S. BONUS: I have created a dedicated resources page on my website, brimming with free resources, blessings, story-behind-the-story clips, and sneak peeks just for you. You can easily access it by visiting the website and clicking on the "Resources" tab.

Moreover, my website friends receive special encouragements, blessings, and plenty of funny memes to lighten the load with each email. If you appreciate being encouraged, blessed, and finding laughter in the lighter side of life, you might have found your people!

Sending much love,
Karen
xxxxx

Have you read others in this series?

Subscribe for the latest information at **karenbrough.com**
Balm for the Exhausted is on its way!

Karen's latest children's book release:

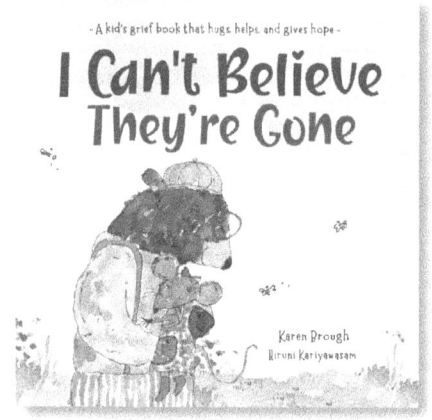

I CAN'T BELIEVE THEY'RE GONE
A Kid's Grief Book that Hugs, Helps and Gives Hope,' now available!

THE LITTLE BLACK CLOUD is on its way!

Subscribe for the news on her latest children's book titles
karenbrough.com

www.ingramcontent.com/pod-product-compliance
Lightning Source LLC
Chambersburg PA
CBHW041312110526
44591CB00022B/2884